J REF   C07 0590 383

KENT ARTS & LIBRARIES

REFERENCE COLLECTION

005467 6   0590 555 78 2

th

D0317385

MEET the AUTHORS and ILLUSTRATORS

60 Creators of Favourite Children's Books

Stephanie Nettell

SCHOLASTIC

To Todd and Barney

Special thanks to Book Trust for their help in the preparation of this book

Each profile in this book lists a short further selection of books by the author or illustrator. The first publisher of each title and the year of first publication are listed. We have tried to make sure this information is correct, and apologise if there are any mistakes.

Scholastic Children's Books,
Scholastic Publications Ltd,
7-9 Pratt Street, London NW1 0AE, UK

Scholastic Inc.,
555 Broadway, New York, NY 10012, USA

Scholastic Canada Ltd,
123 Newkirk Road, Richmond Hill,
Ontario, Canada L4C 3G5

Ashton Scholastic Pty Ltd,
PO Box 579, Gosford, New South Wales,
Australia

Ashton Scholastic Ltd,
Private Bag 92801, Penrose, Auckland,
New Zealand

First published by Scholastic Publications Ltd, 1994

Copyright © Stephanie Nettell, 1994

ISBN: 0 590 55578 2

Printed by E. Baylis

10 9 8 7 6 5 4 3 2 1

All rights reserved.

Stephanie Nettell has asserted her moral right to be identified as the author of the work in accordance with the Copyright, Design and Patents Act 1988.

This book is sold subject to the condition that it shall not, by way of trade or otherwise be lent, resold, hired out, or otherwise circulated without the publisher's prior consent in any form of binding or cover other than that in which it is published and without a similar condition, including this condition, being imposed upon the subsequent purchaser.

KENT
ARTS & LIBRARIES

C070590383

Contents

Introduction

When you look at the names on a book jacket, do you ever wonder what kind of people they are? How they came to earn a living by telling stories or drawing pictures? Were they always special people, brilliant at school, aiming single-mindedly towards a dream? Or did they muddle anxiously through life, waiting to discover if they were good at anything at all?

Here are the life stories of sixty of the most popular creators of children's books, which will answer some of your questions. They are among those men and women whose work is loved, read and re-read, borrowed and bought in tens of thousands by today's children.

Facing over 7,000 new children's books published every year, inevitably I had to leave out many of my own favourites and doubtless many of yours too. (But if this collection proves to have been useful we may do another, so if you long to know more about some particular author or artist, let us know.)

Seven thousand books – what riches! When I and many of the people in this book were growing up, there were only 1,500 titles in a year, and even fewer during the war. No one came to talk to *us* in school. On my eleventh birthday I was given *The Hills of Varna*, and the nearest I came to recognising a children's writer as a real person was to write – very daringly – to my hero, Geoffrey Trease, for his autograph. Today authors and artists, if they are to get any new work done, must ration the time they spend answering the fan mail and questionnaires that pour through their front doors.

Perhaps these profiles will help. They are intended to round out the person behind a book, prepare the ground before a visit, add personal interest to a piece of project work. They are primarily about the writers' and artists' lives, rather than a literary or technical analysis of their work. If you already enjoy their books, I hope you will be interested in the background that led to their creation; if the books are new to you, I'd like to think you might be intrigued enough to explore them for yourself. At the end of each profile I have suggested a range of more key titles to try.

I have pictured my audience as Middle School age, who, while now on the brink of young adult fiction, can still recall the books they first loved, perhaps before, or just after, they could read. But I hope anyone interested in children's reading – teachers or librarians, booksellers or parents (even, judging by the lack of information, publishers!) – may find something useful and entertaining here, too.

Mostly, however, I would like a young reader to be able to identify with one or two of the people portrayed, to look out for the unexpected twists life can bring, the stroke of luck, the unsuspected talent. For all of us, books and reading are the magic door to a world where anything can happen; the creators of books have a special key to that door. At some point in their lives, they risked having a go and turning it. Why don't you?

Stephanie Nettell
October, 1993

John Agard

What's a poetsonian? John Agard says he's a poetsonian – a poet who feels close ties with Caribbean calypsonians, with all their "satirical wit, folksy surrealism and rhythms of language". And what a performer! Words have always cast a spell on him, he says, and he's passing it on – he toured 2,000 schools during the years of his attachment to the Commonwealth Institute.

No surprise that he started out to be an actor. He was born, "a one-child", in Georgetown, the capital of Guyana, a small country poised between being South American and Caribbean. When he was little, he used to pretend to be a priest chanting Latin or a cricket commentator on the radio, relishing the ritual, drama and special language of both.

By the time he was fifteen and played Captain Hook at his Jesuit secondary school, he was addicted. He later became a member of a Guyanese theatre group, All-ah-We, touring the Caribbean (it had begun as He One, became Dem Two, and grew into All-ah-We with the third member), and he even appeared in a Guyanese film. So he's been a performer all his life.

Yet it turned out it was really the words which mattered. He loved not only elocution and debating but writing, and wrote his first poems at sixteen. He gathered up his A level English, Latin and French and, as a pupil teacher, taught them to O level; he was a library assistant and then a journalist for four years; he was a film scriptwriter and radio presenter. He broadcast some stories, and published for himself a collection of poems and a picture book.

His father had already emigrated to Britain, and, in 1977 when John was twenty-eight and hoping to widen his writing career, he followed. With him was fellow Guyanese poet, Grace Nichols (see page 100), and they have been together ever since. Today they live in Lewes, Sussex, with their young daughter (they each have a grown-up daughter from a previous marriage). Perhaps it was for her that they wrote *No Hickory, No Dickory, No Dock*, their collection of Caribbean nursery rhymes – both traditional and ones they wrote themselves.

But of course it was for all children. Words, for John, have magic no matter what "language" they are in. He knows that kids who normally speak and read only conventional English enjoy the sparkle, the fun and the rhythm of his Creole English (the language spoken in various forms throughout the English-speaking Caribbean) as much as he and his A level classmates responded to the poems of Wordsworth, even though they themselves wouldn't be able to do a Lake District accent.

He writes in both straight English and Creole. *Letters for Lettie*, his first children's stories in this country, was written with "correct" grammar, although vivid phrases kept creeping in ("the postman had a bouncy sweet-boy way of walking"), while *I Din Do Nuttin*, a book of poems, is bilingual. Why? Because, he says, the language is organic, the inner spirit which you can't pin down, and can't be separated from the poem.

Both his adult work and children's have won awards, and in 1992 he was appointed the first poet-in-residence at London's South Bank arts complex. He believes poetry should delight, and travels all over the world to make sure it does. He doesn't drive and, like many writers in this book, treasures train journeys. "Train windows are an excellent space for letting thoughts drift in stillness and movement – especially when accompanied by a drop of Guinness."

SELECTED TITLES

I Din Do Nuttin
(The Bodley Head), 1983

The Calypso Alphabet
(HarperCollins), 1990

Laughter is an Egg
(Kestrel), 1990

The Emperor's Dan Dan
(Hodder & Stoughton), 1992

The Great Snakeskin
(verse play)
(Ginn), 1993

The Monster Who Hated Balloons
(Longman), 1994

Janet and Allan Ahlberg

Everybody loves the Ahlbergs! Kids, of course, but also their parents and, more amazingly, the critics: almost all the top children's book awards have tumbled at their feet. The peculiar chemistry that draws two people together sparked off for Janet and Allan not just an emotional but a creative partnership, and a breathtakingly successful one, too – over a hundred titles sell in their millions in a dozen different languages.

"I suppose," says Allan, "that if we hadn't met, neither of us might have got the chance to do what we really wanted. It's like a lyricist meeting a composer. Put them together and they can make songs, but apart they can't make anything." Emotionally this may be true, but Allan has actually written many stories (like *Woof!*, where a boy turns into a dog) and poems (like *Please Mrs Butler*, which gives such a funny and touching view of school life) with other artists, and Janet is a skilled illustrator in her own right.

But meet they did, at a teacher training college in Sunderland. Having already tried being a postman, a gravedigger and a plumber, Allan then became a primary school teacher for ten years, and even a Head in Oxfordshire. But Janet hated teaching. "It's all right if you're not shy as I am, otherwise it's like having to go on stage every day." Instead, she studied graphic design at Leicester School of Art, and worked as a layout artist on women's magazines, illustrated non-fiction books and designed things out of yogurt pots – which was fun but scarcely a career.

No one gave her stories to illustrate, so she asked

Allan to write one (he had been trying since the age of twelve, but could never finish anything). As a teacher, he had noticed that there were not many books for boys of nine or ten who couldn't read very well, so together they produced *The Brick Street Boys* in 1976. The number of titles clocked up rapidly because many come in series like *Happy Families* for new readers, or *Funnybones*, about the daft antics of a big and little skeleton and their skeleton dog.

Allan grew up in a Birmingham working-class terrace in the 1940s. "The baby in *Peepo!* is really me, in a pretty version of the grubby street and the house with the tin bath in front of the fire." Janet, six years younger, grew up in Leicester and that's where they eventually settled, in a Victorian house that allows them to work closely as one unit yet separately – Janet likes the radio, Allan doesn't.

Jessica was born in 1979, and gave them lots of ideas – she liked playing with mail order catalogues (*The Baby's Catalogue*) and, what proved best of all, taking the post in and out of its envelopes. *The Jolly Postman* broke new ground in book design and took five years to get right. "It was nightmarish for the publisher." The Ahlbergs take an obsessively keen interest in all the production details of their books – the balance of words and pictures, the width of margin, size of type, the paper, the colour printing, even the book-jacket's blurb.

Alone, Allan's work is often contemporary, but their teamwork tends to match inventive designs and chirpy playground-talk with traditional comic book symbols – burglars, steamboat captains, First World War pilots. So they blend the old with the new in a world suspended between the Edwardian era and the forties, an almost-real world peopled with characters from classic tales and nursery rhymes, lively, comforting and very funny.

SELECTED TITLES

The Vanishment of Thomas Tull (A&C Black), 1977

The Ha Ha Bonk Book (Viking), 1982

Ten in a Bed (Granada), 1983

Starting School (Viking), 1988

Heard It in the Playground (Viking), 1989

The Bear Nobody Wanted (Viking), 1992

Bernard Ashley

Bernard Ashley's home is three-quarters of a mile from where he was born in 1935, in Woolwich, south-east London, one mile from Charlton Manor Junior School, where he is Head, and right at the heart of the Thames-side world he writes about. His wife is also from Charlton and also a teacher, and two of his three sons are teachers – one of them, Chris, even writes children's books.

But life is never so precisely contained. Evacuated to Preston away from the Docklands' bombing, Bernard eventually collected fourteen different primary schools; later he did National Service in the RAF, studied education at Hertford and Cambridge, and taught in Kent, Herts and London's East End before coming home to roost in 1977.

He's a vigorous, down-to-earth sort of chap, with a chortling guffaw and an instinctive understanding of what it's like to be young: "Old and bald though I am, a lot of my reactions are still a seventeen-year-old's!" In all his stories, whether for infants or teenagers, he deals comfortingly with some real worry – losing your dinner money or wetting the bed, ruining your watch swimming or dodging local criminals, translating English for your parents or enduring secret beatings. But that's not his main purpose: he offers entertainment in fast action and thought-provoking ideas, not "medicine writing", which he scorns.

It was his strong characters and plots that brought his work to television. The Children's Film Foundation filmed *Terry on the Fence* in 1985 (he thinks these days he would put in less description), but as an experiment he wrote *Running Scared* as a script for BBC TV before turning it into an equally successful novel, and *The Country Boy* was published as an original script simultaneously with its appearance on television. Producing a book from a script is fascinating as a craft, but lacks the sheer fun of telling himself a story where he doesn't know the ending – the writing becomes a bit like homework.

In all Bernard Ashley's books, even for the youngest readers, there is an awareness of the society in which his characters have to live. There are both mums and dads coping on their own; there are the scars of racial hatred, mixed marriages, and cultural tug-of-wars between the generations; there's unemployment and lack of money, cruelty and crime – "I'm lucky to know some police who speak the language of crooks!" But there is also humour, and an unsentimental warmth and love – his work is realistic and hopeful, never depressing.

In mid-career he made a special educational study of immigrant children, then took the headship of a large multi-racial school in East Ham – "my *A Kind of Wild Justice* period." Although it is clear, he says, that he's "coming from the left", he steers away from politics.

He used to worry about parents who might think, insultingly, that he couldn't run a school and write books, but now he realises that if he didn't write he couldn't do the job. "One of my favourite quotes is from W.H. Auden, that 'man needs escape as he needs food and deep sleep' – writing is my way of escape. It adds a dimension to my life."

He gives his school a copy of each novel as a thank you for all the exercise books he takes from the stockroom. "At first, the kids used to sidle up to me: 'Mr Ashley, is your first name Bernard?' Television made the difference: now they may even be a little bit proud of me."

SELECTED TITLES

The Trouble with Donovan Croft (Oxford), 1974

Break in the Sun (Oxford), 1980

Dodgem (Julia MacRae), 1981

Clipper Street Stories (Orchard), 1987-9

Seeing Off Uncle Jack (Viking), 1991

Dockside School Stories (Walker), 1992

AUTHOR

Lynne Reid Banks

Rashly, in order to stop her eight-year-old son moaning about the bathroom's grotty medicine cabinet – "There's no magic about new things, Omri!" – his mother had promised a bedtime story about it, and was frantically casting round for ideas.

Perhaps it could bring things to life? How about that little plastic Indian lying by Omri's bed? He was a chief, but Lynne Reid Banks, Omri's mother, instinctively knew she'd need room to develop him, so she downgraded him to a brave. She wanted Omri to really believe, so she built the story round himself, their own terrace house in Kew, and his own friend Patrick. For the next fortnight he couldn't get to bed fast enough.

But she forgot all about Little Bull until years later when she was stuck for ideas and Omri reminded her of him. Published in 1981, *The Indian in the Cupboard* took three years to take off; then it became a best seller, won awards and changed her life – just as *The L-Shaped Room*, her first adult novel, had years before.

Success brought not only three sequels, but allowed earlier, almost forgotten, books to be reissued, like the lovely fairy-tale adventure, *The Farthest-Away Mountain* (from 1976, though written before she had published anything). But it was a surprise. She thinks *I, Houdini* (told by a hilariously pompous little hamster) is a better book, while *Sarah and After*, one of the few still out of print, remains her favourite.

Opinions, memories and, above all, stories simply flow out of Lynne Reid Banks. She has been writing since she was tiny, though her strong presence, clear voice, and hair drawn back like a ballet dancer's suggest her early ties with the stage. Her many titles range from her first young illustrated book, *The Adventures of King Midas* (now rewritten for older readers) to teenage romantic fantasies like *Melusine*, from folk tales to studies of the Brontës.

She was born in Barnes, south-west London, where her father was a doctor. Her mother, a beautiful actress who had sacrificed her career to be his wife, was evacuated with Lynne and her cousin to the Canadian prairies during the war. Lynne returned at fifteen, profoundly marked by being away — by the difference in herself and in England, and particularly by the newsreels she saw of the Nazi death camps. She became captivated by Israel and all things Jewish.

She refused to return to school, but trained as a secretary and at the Royal Academy of Dramatic Art, then worked in the theatre for five years. After a brief diversion to journalism and playwriting, she joined the new commercial TV channel as one of the first two women reporters on ITN. *The L-Shaped Room* was written in quiet moments there. In 1962 she joined Chaim Stephenson, an Israeli sculptor, on a kibbutz where she lived for eight years, and there her three sons were born.

Israel is the setting for novels like *One More River* and *Children at the Gate*, and in 1979 she published *Letters to my Israeli Sons*, a moving historical survey for her teenage boys of their native country.

Now their sons have grown up, and they themselves live in a cottage in Dorset, bright with folk art from around the world and Chaim's sculptures, with their workrooms in a converted farm-building surrounded by ducks and hens.

But keep an eye on your school gate. In Israel she taught English and discovered a lifelong joy: wherever she finds herself in the world, India, Africa, America or Britain, she searches longingly for a classroom, eager to set young minds on fire.

SELECTED TITLES

The Indian in the Cupboard quartet (Dent), from 1980

Maura's Angel (Dent), 1984

The Fairy Rebel (Dent), 1985

Melusine (Hamish Hamilton), 1988

The Adventures of King Midas (HarperCollins), 1993

The Magic Hare (HarperCollins), 1993

Nina Bawden

A bookshop assistant once said that Nina Bawden was one of the few authors whose picture on a book jacket attracts readers rather than puts them off. Indeed, she is the most elegantly attractive grandmother any grandchild – and she has nine – could wish for. The most disconcertingly clear-sighted, too, because both her adult novels and her children's reveal a keen memory of the feelings of childhood.

Today she lives in a tall terrace house on the banks of the Regent's Canal in Islington, north London (the setting of *The Robbers*), although she and her husband, the former Managing Director of the BBC World Service, enviably spend every spring and autumn in Nauplion, the first capital of independent Greece.

She's a Londoner, born and bred near Ilford. Her father, who was half-Italian and half-Scottish, was Chief Engineer on a passenger liner (and an armed merchant cruiser in the war), and so was away for most of the time, leaving Nina and her two younger brothers alone with their mother, Judy. She was a teacher from Swaffham in Norfolk.

Judy's own mother, a dressmaker, used to tell stories of their life at the turn of the century, when her husband had gone to America and she had had to struggle to care for the children. As poor families often did then, they kept a pig on left-over scraps. His name was Johnny. It was out of these early stories that *The Peppermint Pig* developed.

Nina was a young teenager when the Second World War began. While her mother and the boys went to live on a Shropshire farm, she was evacuated with her school to Aberdare, in South Wales, where she lived in term-time with different families – mostly miners', but also a chemist's above the shop – but spent the holidays on the farm.

The memory of these years lies behind *Carrie's War* and *Keeping Henry* – Henry the little red squirrel that lived with them on the farm. *The White Horse Gang* is also set in Shropshire, but, as in all stories, facts and real-life events were melted down, remoulded, rearranged and looked at from new angles in order to create a piece of crafted fiction.

Nina Bawden says she remembers being a child who had extremely strong feelings which she was not encouraged to express – and, of course, couldn't when she was living in someone else's house. She was always writing stories, poems and plays, usually about children enduring some grave injustice in a cruel world. As soon as she had left Oxford (with a degree in Philosophy, Politics and Economics), she wrote her first novel, an adult thriller. Several novels later she realised that her recollection in them of childhood emotions was so clear that writing for children themselves seemed an obvious step.

So when her own children, two boys and a girl, found a secret passage in the cellar of the old house they lived in that led next door (yes, it does sound too good to be true), she wrote *The Secret Passage* especially for them. Now she has written more than twenty adult novels (she appears on Booker Prize shortlists, and was elected a Fellow of the Royal Society of Literature in 1970) and about as many children's, tending to alternate them year by year. Sometimes they inter-relate, and one book explores the childhood of an adult character in another.

"The things I write about for adults," she says, "I write about for children, too: emotions, motives, the difficulties of being honest with oneself, the gulf between what people say and what they really mean."

SELECTED TITLES

Carrie's War
(Gollancz), 1973

The Peppermint Pig
(Gollancz), 1975

Keeping Henry
(Gollancz), 1988

The Outside Child
(Gollancz), 1989

Humbug
(Gollancz), 1992

The Real Plato Jones
(Hamish Hamilton), 1994

AUTHOR

Ian Beck

For over thirty years Britain has produced the best picture books in the world. One reason for this goes back to a time when it was natural for magazines and adult books to be illustrated by the greatest artists of their day, and when this practice died (except for expensive fine-art publishing), more of these fine artists turned to children's books.

They were poorly paid, however, and newly graduated artists had to look for other ways to earn a decent living. Some themselves taught in art schools, others turned to the more profitable business of promoting products with advertisements, shop interiors and packaging. When, in the last fifteen years, publishers treated artists more fairly, it became rarer for new children's book illustrators to have come through this route.

Ian Beck is one of these rare ones. He was already an established and internationally acclaimed commercial designer when he produced his first baby's picture book, *Round and Round the Garden,* in 1982. He is also one of the few modern artists whose work decorates special editions of adult classics.

He was born in the seaside town of Hove, in Sussex. He was thirteen, and on holiday on the Isle of Wight, when he saw an exhibition of drawings for the *Radio Times* – a journal which, like *Punch,* was once a regular showcase for top artists. This so excited him that he began Saturday painting classes at his local College of Art in Brighton, and at fifteen he left school to go there for two foundation years (he was below age) before studying graphic design and illustration. And he was already collecting old illustrated books for children, simply as lovely objects.

He graduated in 1968. He had hit a period when

some of our most distinguished children's illustrators – Raymond Briggs, John Lawrence, Justin Todd and John Vernon Lord – were teaching there, and when British picture books were capturing the world. Yet after all this, Ian climbed another ladder.

A 1970 poster for James Taylor began a long association with Warner Brothers Records, designing ads and record sleeves – such as Elton John's 1973 *Goodbye Yellow Brick Road*. For years, he designed for Habitat and the Conran Group, including murals for a restaurant in the new Terminal Four at Gatwick.

He has been a leading designer for all sorts of projects, both everyday and collectors' items, has exhibited watercolours in specialist shows about, say, gardens or theatre, and illustrated most magazines and newspapers. Only "a species of pastel fantasy" in his work suggested a future in children's books.

Then a coincidence. He was offered the rhymes of *Round and Round the Garden* to illustrate in 1981, just when his first son was born, and he started to understand what made pictures important from a child's point of view, not a designer's. Now he has two sons and a daughter, and he thinks his books have grown with his children. *The Teddy Robber* was the first with his own text, and its success encouraged the more ambitious *Emily and the Golden Acorn*.

The clinching idea for this fantasy about a sailing ship came when he was washing up, looking out of the window of his home in Richmond, Surrey, at the children playing in their back-garden tree. Richmond, with its houses of red Edwardian brick and streets that are sometimes flooded by the Thames, was an important part of the book, but Ian hopes that what it and all his books have to say "will appeal to children far and wide from this garden and this river, and even the remembered seaside of my childhood."

SELECTED TITLES

The Teddy Robber (Doubleday), 1989

Emily and the Golden Acorn (Doubleday), 1992

Poems for Christmas, edited by Jill Bennett (André Deutsch Children's Books), 1992

Five Little Ducks (Orchard), 1992

Orchard Book of Fairy Tales, with Rose Impey, 1992

Picture Book (André Deutsch Children's Books), September 1994

AUTHOR • ILLUSTRATOR

Photograph: Hamish Hamilton Ltd

James Berry

When James Berry was a little boy he just knew that the life he saw around him was not how the world should be. He was the fourth child in a family of six, growing up on the Caribbean island of Jamaica, in a coastal village on the site of an old plantation slave estate. He himself was born only three generations away from slavery.

Nothing was taught about slavery, there was no political discussion, and in everything that was ever written or said there was a colonial assumption that white people were superior and always good, while black people were always bad and lazy. Yet he could see for himself that the people around him were ordinary, decent and hard-working – it didn't make sense, and he felt frustrated and angry.

By the time he was ten he was dreaming of finding a language in which he could express himself. His education was skimpy, no one believed in a creative cultural tradition which he could follow ("we had been cut off from Africa, we were cut off from *everywhere*"), there were no worthwhile jobs, no books. So when he came to write, he turned to his only legacy, the Bible and psalms.

At seventeen, a wartime labour scheme in the USA, designed to replace men in the Services, seemed to offer an escape from this oppression. He stayed four years, but American society appalled him: he was always terrified, and believed it "mentally mangled and distorted" its black people. Fifty years later, a Southern voice can still make his stomach churn.

Coming home to his village was heaven, but a claustrophobic heaven, and he soon left again. He arrived in Britain in 1948, utterly alone. The racial discrimination had a polite face, but it was nevertheless entrenched. But he liked London – it had libraries, cheap evening classes (four evenings a week after work "but it was a joy") and record libraries of European music. At last he had books to *read*.

He trained as a telegraphist, and worked happily for twenty-six years in the overseas section of the Post Office's Cable and Wireless. There were few black people around in the early days. He gravitated towards "where things were happening" – Brixton, where he lived, the Earl's Court student centre, where everyone was writing, arguing, talking and listening, watching independence come to Africa and to the Caribbean – gave public poetry readings and was determined to take part in social life.

He married an Englishwoman. One day, "the happiest of my life", he was made redundant – now he could really write! He began publishing poetry, short stories, BBC plays, still campaigning for a multicultural society and education, and running writing workshops. Fifteen years ago he moved to Brighton.

James Berry feels compelled to celebrate the Caribbean, knowing that such writing never existed when he was young, and that there was still little when he became writer-in-residence at Vauxhall Manor Comprehensive. He edited *Bluefoot Traveller,* the first British anthology of Caribbean poets, and he was the first black writer to win the National Poetry Competition. *A Thief in the Village,* short stories for children, and *When I Dance,* poems for young people written in a combination of English and Caribbean speech, both won top awards.

In 1991 James Berry the poet was honoured with the Order of the British Empire.

What would that little boy of long ago, who lived in one distant corner of the Empire, have said to that? He had, after all, been right: he did have things to say, and there was more than one language waiting for him to say them – to trample down barriers, and bury them.

SELECTED TITLES

A Thief in the Village
(Hamish Hamilton), 1987

When I Dance
(Hamish Hamilton), 1988

Isn't My Name Magical?
(BBC Books), 1991

Anancy-Spiderman
(Walker), 1992

The Future Telling Lady
(Hamish Hamilton), 1992

AUTHOR

21

Malorie Blackman

Malorie Blackman had set her heart on a degree in English and drama from Goldsmiths' College, in order to teach. She had nine O levels, and was about to take her A's.

"Sorry," said the careers teacher, "I can't give you a reference – I don't think you'll get your English A level. Try business studies at Huddersfield Polytechnic." So she did. But she made sure she got her three A levels, and a "B" in English.

A pity the postman can't deliver a huge parcel of Blackman books to that teacher – although Malorie is too busy writing and too amiable (she peals with laughter when talking about herself) to be bothered with such nonsense. Was the teacher's reaction because she was a girl, or because she was a black girl?

Malorie Blackman is a Londoner, although her parents and the oldest of her three brothers and one sister were born in Barbados (like little Betsey Biggalow). Born in 1962, she's lived almost all her life south of the Thames, settling in Lewisham. She went to Honor Oak Grammar School before obediently tackling business studies in Huddersfield. She hated it. Recuperating from appendicitis in her first term, she asked herself, "Why am I doing this?" – and got a Goldsmiths' place after all.

Meanwhile, however, she worked for a software house and discovered computers; she enjoyed it so much she changed direction to study computer science (with distinction) at Thames Polytechnic. For three years she worked during the day and studied in the evening – it was tough, but she loved it. "Computers and programming had the same neat, disciplined appeal for me as logic puzzles and detective stories, and later at Reuters I wrote software to communicate with machines all round the world. It was a real eye-opener."

It was only when, as a database manager, she was dealing with money markets that she began to feel uncomfortable. She tried classes in acting – no, that wasn't her. "I'd always written short stories and poems, so in 1987 I went to evening classes at the City Lit (Literary Institute)." This was her starting-block, as it has been for so many British authors: she chose writing for children, and her tutor encouraged her to go for publication. After "dozens of well-deserved rejection slips", she was accepted.

With her partner Neil's encouragement (and vital financial subsidy), Malorie gave up work in 1990 to write all day. She aims at three books a year – picture books, short stories and novels – and has already chalked up almost twenty. Predictably, she's inseparable from her word processor, and computers rule OK in one of her most successful novels, *Hacker*.

She writes tirelessly, for the fun of it, and because it's a good excuse to eavesdrop and be nosy! But there is also a kind of *anti*-mission.

"Every Saturday as a child I went to the library (at home we had a set of Encyclopaedia Britannica and that was *it*), and I can't remember one book with a black central character. As a Volunteer Reading Helper in schools I found children longed for *ordinary* stories – where's the *Narnia* with black children? Too often books reinforce the notion that if you're black you have A Problem. But the story, not the *issue*, is what's important."

So she decided, instead of whingeing, she would do something about it. Perhaps it's the memory of that teacher which makes her always say, "If you really want to do something, you must do it!"

SELECTED TITLES

Not So Stupid! (Women's Press), 1990

Girl Wonder series (Gollancz), 1991

Elaine, You're a Brat (Orchard), 1991

Betsey Biggalow series (Piccadilly Press), from 1992

Hacker (Doubleday), 1992

Operation Gadgetman (Doubleday), 1993

AUTHOR

Quentin Blake

Most picture book artists, in their hearts, prefer to illustrate their own stories. Rightly or wrongly, the world sees it as a greater achievement; the artist need not worry about how to interpret someone else's ideas; and it doubles the money. But Quentin Blake actually *likes* illustrating other people's stories.

He has worked with some of our best writers: Joan Aiken (stories about Arabel and the raven Mortimer, made famous by *Jackanory*), Russell Hoban (crazily inventive fantasies), John Yeoman (who has written books specially for him for more than thirty years, and with whose gentle fun and wit he is particularly in tune), J.P. Martin (the wonderful *Uncle* stories), Michael Rosen (the always bouncy poet) and, of course, in famous partnership with Roald Dahl. He says illustrating different people's words and ideas is stimulating because it means there are so many things going on.

He works with the best because he too is the best. He is possibly the only artist many children could name – and children as young as four can recognise when a drawing is his, even if they don't know his name. (Talking of names, French children, who love him too, call him "Contang Black".) His own stories are just as popular, and win just as many prizes, from his first, *Patrick*, in 1968, to classics like *Mister Magnolia*.

Quentin Blake grew up in Sidcup, in Kent "but really a London suburb", in the 1930s. He has drawn for as long as he can remember, and even while still at school he was sending cartoons off to *Punch* magazine. When he had two accepted – he was only sixteen – he was following in the steps of many of the greatest illustrators of the past.

No one else in his family was an artist, and they would never have expected him to earn a living as one. Indeed, exams, National Service and then studying English at Cambridge University, all interfered with his art, but his cartoons continued to appear in *Punch*, and after taking a teaching diploma in London he studied part-time at Chelsea School of Art.

His cartooning gradually turned into illustration – for journals like *The Spectator* and *The Listener* as well as adult books – and his last drawing for *Punch* was a jacket cover in 1988, forty years after his first. He never was a school teacher, but in 1965 he was appointed a tutor at the Royal College of Art in London, and in 1978 became Head of the Illustration Department for eight years. Now he is an honorary visiting professor, which leaves him time to stay in his house in France. His real home has always been in the Earl's Court district of London, where an art teacher at his school had lived and whose flat he had admired for its airy rooms and big windows.

Looking back, he realises he could have made a living from his art alone, but he enjoys teaching, and the way it makes you think about things. And that diploma proved useful. "Teaching properly is not just about conveying information. You must present things in a way that will get a certain audience reaction, as in the theatre, and that's what you do in books, too – they are all related.

"There are two kinds of detail: the masses of detail children can pore over, and *significant* detail. I don't put in a lot of stuff" (a skill derived from cartoons), "but children still think there is detail. I layer in things which they can react to, I trail things – just as in the classroom."

SELECTED TITLES

How Tom Beat Captain Najork and His Hired Sportsmen, with Russell Hoban
(Cape), 1974

The Enormous Crocodile, with Roald Dahl
(Cape), 1978

Mrs Armitage on Wheels
(Cape), 1987

All Join In
(Cape), 1990

Cockatoos
(Cape), 1992

Quentin Blake: An Album
(Cape), 1994

AUTHOR • ILLUSTRATOR

Judy Blume

Photograph copyright © Katie Vandyck, 1993

Judy Blume is famous for being many things – funny, wise, pretty, sympathetic – but her moral courage is often forgotten.

In America her books have sometimes been banned from libraries. She often felt isolated, because her staggeringly high sales mean some sections of a jealous literary establishment are unwilling to support her. But she fought back, and when she declared, "We have to look at what we're saying to children when we take a book off the shelf: 'If you don't like someone's ideas, get rid of them'," she was making a fundamental statement about freedom. Even in her fun questionnaire for fans, she lists her pet hates as intolerance and prejudice.

When she visited Britain a few years ago, the newspapers and radio deliberately rekindled controversy about her love story *Forever*, which she had written to explain sexual responsibility to her daughter. This irritated her, because it was published here way back in 1976, and was meant for young adults, anyway, not children. She says to anxious parents, "Read it yourselves, then talk about it, and the characters, to your children. There's no law that prevents your saying to them, 'In our family, this is not acceptable behaviour'."

It also takes courage to tackle, not just the thousands of letters each month from readers all over the world, but the often desperate problems they contain. In 1981, in response to such letters, Judy established the Kids Fund, to which she directs royalties from her books. It gives grants to charitable bodies that help young people cope with growing up in our modern society.

When she gathered the letters together in *Letters to*

Judy, they produced ten times as many painful new ones as ever before! Her special readers at her publishers could only bear them for an hour at a time. Since they're a month old by the time she gets them, she feels miserably powerless to help the urgent ones. To leave any time to write, she has learnt to protect herself from her own emotions, remembering that it was because of her books that they wrote in the first place.

What has made her happy is hearing from readers who are now old enough to be shop assistants joyfully recognising her credit card signature in every New York store, or to be even parents themselves (*she's a grandmother!*).

She had married her first husband, attorney John Blume, while at college, and was already expecting her daughter when she graduated. When her younger child (the original Fudge) went to nursery school, she thought of writing, and attended courses at New York University for encouragement. Her first novel, *Iggie's House*, was published in 1968 when she was thirty, after two years of rejected efforts. It was *Are You There God? It's Me, Margaret* which made her feel she might really be a writer.

Like Margaret, she grew up in a New Jersey suburb; she lived with her second husband in New Mexico before moving back to New York City, and she sets her books in these familiar backgrounds. "Writing about young people wasn't a conscious decision, it was what I knew best. I remembered everything about being ten, eleven and twelve. Of all my characters I am most like Margaret Simon and Sally Freedman. And I had all of Sheila Tubman's fears.

"I get very angry at adults who tell me they want to protect their children from the real world. I try to be honest in my books. I think all people, young and old, want to know that others share their feelings. That no matter what, they're not alone."

SELECTED TITLES

Otherwise Known as Sheila the Great
(The Bodley Head), 1978

Deenie
(Heinemann), 1980

Tiger Eyes
(Heinemann), 1982

The Pain and the Great One
(Heinemann), 1985

Just as Long as We're Together
(Heinemann), 1987

Fudge-a-Mania
(The Bodley Head), 1991

Raymond Briggs

"**W**hen you go to art school," says Raymond Briggs, "all the uncles and aunts say, 'Oh, there's no money in art, you shouldn't let him do that,' and then you make more money than the rest put together." Actually, money isn't important enough to him to make him gloat, but it's a satisfying thought.

And as a working-class boy, he knows money's useful. He was born in Wimbledon Park, south London, in 1934, and his dad was a Co-op milkman – like Father Christmas, he hated winter mornings. Boys in Briggs's books often look like Raymond (especially in *The Man*), and a recurring figure in his work, a rather touching back view of an ordinary working bloke, is based on his father.

At first Raymond wanted to be a newspaper reporter, then, when he began drawing seriously at thirteen, a cartoonist – like so many other artists, he was influenced by *Punch* magazine. When he was fifteen he began a four-year painting course at Wimbledon School of Art, "a very old-fashioned traditional training" which believed art had been going steadily downhill since 1880, but good for an illustrator.

He spent his National Service entirely at Catterick Camp in Yorkshire and managed to do some painting. One of his pictures was so well reviewed, it gave him the idea he was going to be a famous painter. If he could get that far with an army painting, what would a Slade training do? At twenty-three he left the Slade School of Fine Art convinced he was no painter, but realising he could "draw and paint from imagination and memory" – exactly what *illustration* is all about.

He began by both illustrating and writing fairly run-of-the-mill younger stories. In 1961 he started his twenty-six years as a part-time lecturer at Brighton College of Art, and in 1963 he married the painter, Jean Taprell Clark, who died of leukaemia ten years later. By then he was working on *Fee Fi Fo Fum*, a book of nursery rhymes which heralded his future classic, *The Mother Goose Treasury* (1966), whose 897 briskly jolly pictures, rebelling against sugary prettiness for babies, won his first Kate Greenaway Medal (*Father Christmas* won the second).

Raymond Briggs publishes a title only every few years. This is partly by choice, and partly because he is also designing and writing for the theatre and radio and working on films. But mainly it is because the hundreds of frames in the strip cartoon format entail a huge burden of work – every time someone speaks you have to *draw* them.

Briggs is the acknowledged king of this underrated art-form in Britain, experimenting with the design of each page and challenging it to say something memorable to readers of any age – whether for fun like *Fungus the Bogeyman*, or with trenchant passion, like *The Tin-Pot Foreign General and the Old Iron Woman* or *When the Wind Blows*.

"The graphic design of a book is the hard part – writing is the easy, enjoyable bit. I begin with a fantasy situation and then play it straight. Nuclear war next week, a tiny man suddenly appearing, a snowman coming to life: right, now what happens? And even if it's pretty gloomy, in the last resort it must be funny too."

What happens is that his characters take on their own immortal existence in the world's imagination (the merchandising, he says, has got quite out of control). So down in Hassocks, in the winding lane tucked under the Sussex Downs where he has lived for so long, Raymond Briggs finds something else to do while *The Snowman* gets another Christmas outing.

SELECTED TITLES

The Mother Goose Treasury
(Hamish Hamilton), 1966

Father Christmas
(Hamish Hamilton), 1973

Fungus the Bogeyman
(Hamish Hamilton), 1977

The Snowman
(Hamish Hamilton), 1978

When the Wind Blows
(Hamish Hamilton), 1982

The Man
(Julia MacRae), 1992

AUTHOR • ILLUSTRATOR

Anthony Browne

Anthony Browne says that as a child he drew pictures very like the ones he draws now, but they were on *big* pieces of paper (suitable for battle scenes) and they were full of details and jokes, and arrows to point out what was happening. But surrealism (the unexpected odd happenings you get in dreams) was always there.

He has no idea where it came from, only that he felt a shock of recognition when he discovered "official" examples, like *Alice in Wonderland* when he was nine, or the artist Magritte when he was fourteen. He hadn't realised other people, too, had been in his strange world. So of all the modern artists illustrating *Alice*, he is surely the most at home.

He's a Yorkshire lad, born in Sheffield and brought up near Halifax, who thought he might be a cartoonist, a newspaper reporter, or even a boxer. Although he is not very big (or perhaps *because* he was slight and liked drawing), he was very sporty, and until he was thirty he was a keen rugby scrum-half. In the end he went to Leeds College of Art for a degree in graphic design (a course which in those days was geared to advertising, and he hated it), and later became a medical artist at Manchester Royal Infirmary.

Now he can see what fine training this was for picture books. Not just for technical drawing and water colours, but because an artist has to tell what is *really* going on in a hospital operation in a way photographs never could. "You have to concentrate very hard and show what is actually happening – but not in a completely realistic way. The liver, for instance, looks just a mess, so you have to paint it *cleaned up*, looking as people imagine liver – so it *looks* real. And that's the same as in, say, *Piggybook:* a living room *seems* real, but actually it isn't when you look carefully."

For fifteen years he designed Gordon Fraser greetings cards; he enjoyed it, and it provided a regular income, but inevitably the same ideas began appearing. He gave up while he was working on *Alice* (published in 1988) and never returned. But cards alone had never been sufficient, so he tried publishing as an experiment – he had forgotten he used to make up stories when he was young.

"My editor at Hamish Hamilton, Julia MacRae, taught me everything: how to plan a book, to make a dummy and discuss it rather than offer a finished product, and how pictures and words can work together." His first book, *Through the Magic Mirror*, which appeared in 1976 when he was thirty, was instantly recognised as a mature, skilled and intriguingly individual piece of work. There is no other artist quite like him.

He rarely does more than one or two books a year; the *Little Bear* stories may take about six weeks, a major book about a year, and *Piggybook*, which started life very differently ("deeply depressing" because the mother leaves in disgust and never comes back!), was put aside for two years to develop.

He lives near Canterbury now. His wife Jane is a professional violinist and pianist, as well as an artist herself (you can glimpse someone curiously like Anthony in her book, *My Wicked Stepmother*, and someone curiously like Jane in *Piggybook*). Both children are not only musical but their son (who is a scrum-half too) writes and illustrates his own stories.

"One was even published in an anthology and illustrated by Posy – do you think one day he'll write stories for me?"

SELECTED TITLES

Bear Hunt
(Hamish Hamilton), 1979

Gorilla
(Julia MacRae), 1983

Willy the Wimp series
(Julia MacRae), from
1984

Piggybook
(Julia MacRae) 1986

Alice in Wonderland,
by Lewis Carroll
(Julia MacRae), 1988

Zoo
(Julia MacRae), 1992

AUTHOR • ILLUSTRATOR

John Burningham

There is a certain house with a strong character that looks out one way on to Hampstead Heath and out the other to a vast garden. It feels partly like a lordly manor and partly like a sunny farmhouse – you would never believe you were in London.

Two artists live there: up at the top of the house used to be Helen Oxenbury's studio (see page 102), although these days she has a separate one away from home, while down at garden level is John Burningham's. Since their grown-up son and daughter are also artists, their younger girl, who still lives at home, must once have supposed the world was made of artists.

They have "circulated around the area" since John's student days, and Helen says it is John who has made the house and garden amazing. "When we bought it no one would have given tuppence for it! He loves architecture, haunts demolition sites for unexpected finds, is brilliant at designing and making things – he totally transforms everything."

John Burningham was born in 1936 in Surrey, but went to a famously "progressive" school in Suffolk called Summerhill, where lessons are voluntary. It bred the kind of courage needed to be a conscientious objector at seventeen, at a time when two years' military service was compulsory for boys. Instead he served in the Friends Ambulance Unit, and worked in forestry, farming, slum-clearing and school-building in southern Italy and demolition work in Israel. Then, on a friend's advice, and almost accidentally, he went to London's Central School of Art: his final graduation work was an album of drawings created from foot- and hand-prints.

He returned to Israel to design models and puppets for animated films. Home again, he cartooned, did television trailers and Christmas cards, and his posters for London Transport became a familiar sight to tube travellers. But when he carted his portfolio around the publishing companies, wanting to be an illustrator, no one wanted to know. "When you've done a book or two, let us see."

He got fed up and wrote his own. It was *Borka: The Adventures of a Goose With No Feathers* (1963), and it won the Kate Greenaway Medal for children's book illustration. Since then he has produced about two books a year and become world-renowned, won further awards (another Kate Greenaway for *Mr Gumpy's Outing*) and been translated into eleven languages, while *Granpa* has been turned into an internationally popular animated film, just as *Oi! Get Off Our Train* will be.

He was one of a group of adventurous young artists, like Brian Wildsmith, who had a massive impact on children's picture books in the 1960s. After *Borka* came *Trubloff*, the mouse who wanted to play the balalaika, then *Humbert*, a scrap-iron merchant's horse who draws the Lord Mayor of London's coach. To illustrate *Chitty-Chitty-Bang-Bang* in 1964 he made a model car with wings, superimposing and touching up photographs. He was a "painterly" artist in slabs of strong colours, but became a major artist in what is considered to be the most difficult medium, colour line.

His stories are for any age. Some compare what goes on in a young person's imagination with what is happening in the "real" adult world outside, while others fret about what we are doing to our environment. He's a quiet man who doesn't scatter smiles around, but his pictures reveal a world of intense colour, passion and a biting, almost crazy humour appreciated by young readers everywhere.

SELECTED TITLES

Mr Gumpy's Outing
(Cape), 1970

Come Away From the Water, Shirley
(Cape), 1977

Granpa
(Cape), 1984

Oi! Get Off Our Train
(Cape), 1989

Aldo
(Cape), 1991

Harvey Slumfenburger's Christmas Present
(Walker), 1993

AUTHOR • ILLUSTRATOR

Betsy Byars

Betsy Byars sees herself as very uncool: she says it's her nature to overdo everything. "This has been one of the hardest, most unnatural things about my writing – to keep myself from telling too much." She may need curbing, but it's part of a warm, funny personality whose sympathy shines through to her readers.

She surely knows all about discipline. First, a licensed pilot, she is addicted to flying. She was in her last year at college, studying English, when she met her husband, a Professor of Engineering with a 1931 Stinson aeroplane. They've been married over forty years; he has owned about fifty planes in that time, she one. When she planned *Coast to Coast*, he insisted they (and dog Harvey) barnstorm together across America in a 1940 J-3 Piper Cub. An undisciplined pilot doesn't last that long.

Secondly, her writing routine is painstaking. She researches exhaustively around any idea before even beginning. Then she reworks each burst of writing until she's gone from "This is terrible," through "This is still terrible" and "This is not as terrible as it used to be," to "This is getting better" and finally "This is not bad at all." A familiar enough process for a writer, but with her, one book can take a year to write and another to polish into shape.

Betsy began writing in the 1950s, with light-hearted pieces for the *Saturday Evening Post*. She worked on the kitchen table of their small flat amid the hubbub of two daughters – one more and a son followed. Now-forgotten novels came next, but with *The Summer of the Swans* in 1970, the story of a girl and her retarded brother which won one of America's top awards, came lasting acclaim.

Betsy Byars was born in 1928 in North Carolina, where her father was superintendent at a cotton mill. She was a spirited little girl, with a reputation for being adventurous and tough because she kept her fears to herself. But her terror of Bubba, the big brother of her best friend, is still vivid enough to compel her to name all her loathsome characters after him – even the bully in *The Eighteenth Emergency*, who was eventually renamed the hard-sounding Marv Hammerman.

Her ideas are triggered by real events, her own and the ones she rediscovers in her special drawer, crammed with notes and cuttings and beckoning title-pages. The gift-wrapped dime her sister was given for her birthday during the Depression surfaced in *After the Goat Man*; her own nightmare when, aged five, she was picked up to view "Uncle" Joe in his coffin, and her leg kicked the coffin so that Joe's mouth fell open and she saw the rags inside, became Mr Mason's in *The Pinballs*. She calls such oddities her "Good Scraps", and regards them as essential ingredients.

Even more central are such jumping-off points as meeting a fox for a long, still moment (*The Midnight Fox*), or a news bulletin about an old man known as the Goat Man, who was trying to stop a highway going through his house, or a newspaper story about "the Morgantown Monster" in someone's barn that turned out to be a crane lost on migration (*The House of Wings*).

The Byars once lived in West Virginia, but now Betsy works in a log cabin among quiet woods, ten minutes from their home in Clemson, South Carolina. And even here, the arrival of a handsome black snake on the porch can send her rushing to print out another alluring title page: *The Moon and Me*, by Betsy Byars.

SELECTED TITLES

The Eighteenth Emergency
(The Bodley Head), 1974

After the Goat Man
(The Bodley Head), 1975

Blossom Family books
(The Bodley Head), 1986

Bingo Brown books
(The Bodley Head), 1988

Coast to Coast
(The Bodley Head), 1993

McMummy
(The Bodley Head), 1994

AUTHOR

Charles Causley

Launceston, the old capital of Cornwall, has always been home for Charles Causley. Here he was born in 1917, here he went to school – the same school he returned to as a teacher after the war – and here he has lived ever since. Its streets and churches, the games and rhymes of his childhood, thread in and out of his poetry, but they are not the horizons of his world: he is a warm and entertaining man who has travelled widely.

His mother introduced him to the world of poetry. She had left school at twelve able to recite "great swathes of narrative verse" like Macaulay's *Horatius*, and knowing all the old songs from seaside shows – songs which taught him, he says, more about the comedy and tragedy of life than "Hush-a-bye, Baby".

His father, whose service in France in the First World War had left him an invalid, died young in 1924, when Charles was only seven: *Today, I hardly remember my father's face. . . Only the feel of his iron hand in mine* ("Tavistock Goose Fair"). To supplement her war widow's pension his mother cleaned and took in washing for one of the "big" houses, but she was an avid reader whose library books Charles shared.

After the Church elementary school he took the County Scholarship exam, which in those days meant free education for a selected few at grammar school. Just before his sixteenth birthday, his mother, without telling Charles, arranged for him to work in an office instead of staying on. Devastated, he obeyed.

These were the intellectually exciting years of George Orwell and T.S. Eliot, of H.G. Wells and Bertrand Russell, of W.H. Auden and Stephen Spender, and of the first Penguin Books, at sixpence (2$\frac{1}{2}$p) each – but also of the Spanish Civil War and

Nazi rallies in Germany. "I remember coming home, having my dinner and hearing accounts of the bombing of Madrid. You knew it was all going to happen again. It was as if my whole generation was being washed, in an unstoppable flood of events, towards disaster."

He served in the Navy, never without books stuffed into his kitbag, especially the "indispensable" Shakespeare play. In the first year of the war he had optimistically applied for a peacetime place at a teachers' training college. And after six years he finally got his further education.

As a teacher, he "used to set off feeling like a nineteenth-century explorer with a butterfly net." He rejoiced in the children ("They're heroic – I love the way they go flat out at things"), and saw how those who seemed the most unliterary were often the best poets.

Much of the attraction of Charles Causley's poetry lies in its lyrical music. He himself plays the piano (even, long ago, in a dance-band), and in *The Young Man of Cury* he celebrates his old junior school Headmaster, whose harmonium used to lead the whole school through the Cecil Sharp collection of folk songs that have haunted Charles ever since.

One of Britain's most distinguished poets, Causley writes with the same humanity and humour, the same respectful seriousness of intent, for children as for adults. He was one of the first anthologists of modern poetry for young readers. His own collections, from the immortal *Figgie Hobbin* for children (1970), to the definitive *Collected Poems* which saluted his seventy-fifth birthday in 1992, echo with the passions and memories of his life: strong tales simply told and good tunes, the sea and the Cornish countryside, the innocent vulnerability of childhood and the magic of its imagination, and a contempt for all intolerance.

SELECTED TITLES

Figgie Hobbin
(Macmillan), 1970

The Puffin Book of Salt Sea Verse (ed), 1978

The Sun, Dancing
(Viking), 1984

Jack the Treacle Eater
(Macmillan), 1987

The Young Man of Cury
(Macmillan), 1991

All Day Saturday
(Macmillan), 1994

Babette Cole

Babette Cole seems to talk in exclamation marks and italics. Zany and endlessly chatty – breaking off into peals of laughter – she is exactly as you'd expect someone to be who is called Babette and who invents such hilariously way-out books as *Mummy Laid an Egg!*, *The Smelly Book* or *The Trouble with Gran*.

But although she seems chaotic and good for a giggle, she is a formidably hard worker who organises her frenzied life with great discipline. Her home is deep in the Kentish countryside with Benjy Big Boots (whose grandmother was the original Hush Puppy) and all sorts of other dogs, cats and horses. She couldn't live without horses, and breeds and produces them zealously for county shows.

All round the daily routine of the animals (*and* their foaling) she fits in many hours of work to produce two or three picture books a year as well as her own greetings cards. She says she has so many ideas she calls it mental diarrhoea: she throws them all into a drawer and roots them out when she needs them.

All her books are meant for fun – "I wouldn't know how to *start* a serious work!" – but she does take seriously the technique necessary to produce a good picture book. She could draw academically if she wanted to, but she has always worked in her own "grotesque" style.

"I've softened it because it used to frighten people. I thought big noses and horrible monsters hysterically funny, but everyone else was terrified! Slugs, caterpillars – all my life I've drawn slimy things." Some people see her work as "surreal", but to her the world is really like that. "Look at the carvings on Canterbury Cathedral benches, leering little things on the choristers' seats."

She pretends her funny handwriting with knobs on is all she can do, but really it is because she has never found a typeface that actually suits her drawings. She works closely from start to finish with her publisher's production team, checking processes, reproduction and overall design. For instance, she knows that lettering which will be be translated can't be coloured when the background is also coloured because of the extra cost for foreign editions (her humour is international, and her foreign sales enormous). A story takes her half an hour, but the pictures take three months. Once the creative part, the dummy – that is, the first idea and roughly sketched layout for a book – is finished, the artwork becomes a chore, and she says her drawings are not as intricate as they once were.

Her mother saw the name Babette on a gravestone in Jersey, where her parents had moved to after the Second World War. She went to a convent school in Jersey, worked for a while in advertising (so she knew what she *didn't* want to do) before entering Canterbury College of Art, which she hated. She tended to go her own way, and by her third year was producing her own little books about Prom, the pony heroine who was to become a bestseller and who is still a special favourite.

Prom proved too original in 1973 to be accepted by a publisher, and it was only after Babette had worked with the TV team on *Watch With Mother, Ivor the Engine* and *Bagpuss* that she adapted Prom to a different style and became published. Now she has produced dozens of her own books, in addition to occasionally illustrating other people's, and struggles with a fanmail so huge that answering it could easily stop her producing any more.

SELECTED TITLES

Princess Smartypants
(Hamish Hamilton), 1986

The Slimy Book
(Cape), 1986

Promise and the Monster
(HarperCollins), 1988

Tarzanna!
(Hamish Hamilton), 1991

Winni Allfours
(Hamish Hamilton), 1993

Mummy Laid an Egg!
(Cape), 1993

AUTHOR • ILLUSTRATOR

Caroline B. Cooney

Seven years ago, Caroline Cooney, her two teenage daughters and her son, who was about ten, came to live for a year in London because it sounded so romantic – their own home is in Westbrook, Connecticut, a small town on the east coast of the United States. "For the first time in our lives we had no car, but used the tube, buses and trains, and we felt very urban and sophisticated."

Caroline (the middle initial stands for Bruce, her own name before she married) grew up not far from where she lives now, and normally any excitement and adventure in her life is only in her imagination. She feels she must have read several million books (most of which seem to be in her house – covering the walls, lost under the couch, climbing the stairs) and she's published fifty-two. "My world is as populated by people I have imagined as it is by people who exist." She writes every day for several hours and daydreams about it for the rest of the day.

And has done so since she was twelve, when "the best teacher I ever had in my life" used to rip off covers from *The New Yorker* magazine, pass them round, and make everyone write a story about whichever cover they got. By the time she went to college, she was writing her first book. But neither college nor book proved successful, though she tried four of each. She detested all the colleges and "faded fast", never getting near a degree, and her early books – adult novels set in ancient Rome – remained unpublished. "It's a good thing. They were awful!"

Only after she had children did she turn to writing for young people, selling stories to *Seventeen* magazine. "I felt very comfortable with the age-group. The stories were humorous and low-key, and came very easily." Today the renewed interest in historical novels might tempt her to return to writing for adults, but, she says, she still loves her audience of twelve and thirteen-year-olds, who bring an ideal combination of popularity and anonymity. They read everything she writes, and know her name, while her contemporaries do neither.

Horror (*The Cheerleader*), realism (*I'm Not Your Other Half*), suspense (*The Face on the Milk Carton*), romance (*Saturday Night*) – with psychological subtlety, humour and a fast pace, she is successful in them all. "It took me a long time to write well," she says, "and what I learned is that you must write steadily, enjoy yourself, and never give up."

Suspense is her favourite, both to read and write, because "you can count on action." She is sympathetic to the problems of those, like her son, who find reading difficult. While her girls have never stopped reading, her son for years dreaded any schoolwork that involved a book. People like him are in her mind when she makes such rules as "No slow passages, no descriptions of ancestors or home furnishings!"

It works – all over the world. Her stories have been translated into German, French, Dutch, Swedish and Japanese, and she looks forward to letters from readers as the best part of any day. She says the only difference between British and American fan letters is that British addresses are longer and more intriguing.

She paints her life as peaceful and contented. "I have no unfulfilled hopes! Is that not an amazing statement? Every writing daydream I ever had has come true. An early hope was to be assigned as school homework – I laugh every time I think of a teacher assigning pages of me!"

SELECTED TITLES

The Face on the Milk Carton
(Methuen), 1991

The Cheerleader trilogy
(Point Horror, Scholastic), 1992-3

Freeze Tag
(Point Horror, Scholastic), 1993

Saturday Night quartet
(Point Romance, Scholastic), 1993-4

Flight 116 is Down
(Point Fiction, Scholastic), 1994

Forbidden
(Point Fiction, Scholastic), 1994

Helen Cowcher

It remains a dream for most of us, but for Helen Cowcher, work revolves around the two things she enjoys most: painting and travelling. Although she never set out to make it happen, from the moment in 1988 when *Rainforest* startled the world with its hot colours and tense energy, her paintings and her interest in worldwide environmental issues became totally entwined in her books.

She was born and grew up in Cheltenham, and went to Bournemouth Art College for a year before starting three years of graphic design at the Chelsea School of Art. Already as a student she was doing freelance work for educational publishers. Her interest in plants and animals led her to illustrate a lot of material on gardening and natural history; she specialised in very fine and detailed black and white botanical drawings – not a bit like the bold, sweeping patterns of her later books.

For some years life was a matter of hard work and not much money. Then becoming an illustrator for advertising and packaging – the pretty packaging with, say, flowers and seashells of the kind which firms like Marks and Spencer use – meant Helen could afford to take time for her own painting. But she became more and more aware of a conflict between her concerns about the environment and the wasteful demands of the packaging industry.

For one day a week she taught illustration on the graphic design course at Bath – nine years before, when she herself had been a student, illustration was a neglected subject in art schools. She says she loved travelling by train from her home in Streatham, south London, because she could daydream whilst looking out of the window and ideas would surface in her mind. And teaching others made her look outward and then reflect on what she, herself, was doing.

With more time and money came the chance to travel. She spent one Christmas in India with an Indian friend, went back later with her photographer husband who was himself compiling a book, and, "changed for life by her visits", has returned several times since.

Tigress, her third book in 1991, was actually based on a real-life incident in India when she saw a tiger kill a bullock. Yet, perhaps because it touches on the complicated relationship which people in poorer countries must have with their environment, it is the one that most worried people about its "truth". On the other hand, she has never been to the South Pole, and *Antarctica*, with its luminous polar light making patterns in the deep, cold water, was painted while she was cosily tucked up at home – yet everyone says, surely this is how Antarctica really is.

Helen's paintings are not realistically detailed depictions of scenes, but expressions, in graphic terms, of the essence of plants and animals – the *tigerness* of a tiger, the raucous heat of a rainforest – which at the same time create wonderful patterns on the page. For instance, a round-faced penguin chick, as pure in black and white as a company logo, forms a pattern against its upright, long-beaked parents.

She exhibits (and successfully sells) paintings in galleries, often working with environmental groups like Living Earth, who two years ago sent her and twelve other artists to Venezuela. There she lived on a ranch on the savannah – and inevitably got the idea for another children's book.

SELECTED TITLES

Rainforest
(André Deutsch
Children's Books), 1988

Antarctica
(André Deutsch
Children's Books), 1990

Tigress
(André Deutsch
Children's Books), 1991

Whistling Thorn
(André Deutsch
Children's Books), 1993

AUTHOR • ILLUSTRATOR

Helen Cresswell

Photograph copyright © Newsphoto Chronicle Advertiser, Newgate Lane, Mansfield

Helen Cresswell likes to tell a story about how she shocked two tiny old ladies at a noisy publishing party. She's very tall, and she could only half-hear them asking her something. ". . . how many. . . children. . .?" She thought that, like most people, they were asking her how many children's books she had written.

"It sounds awful, but I've lost count," she said, but added when she saw their horrified expressions, "it must be sixty or seventy, I suppose." They turned and fled.

If she'd heard properly, she could have answered, "Two daughters, the elder of whom is a television producer." But, with an amazing fifty books still in print, maybe the first answer is more impressive.

Since she was seven, Helen Cresswell has never wanted to be anything but a writer. One of the favourite authors of her childhood, Walter de la Mare, has been a clear influence on her own magical fantasies, such as *Moondial*. She says she writes in a "timeless, classic way", and could never be "trendy".

She lives in an old farmhouse not far from Nottingham, having been born and grown up in its suburbs, but identifies so strongly with the North that she directs her TV aerial towards Yorkshire. She studied English at King's College in London in the early 1950s, and only a few brief jobs interfered with the steady march towards being a writer.

She helped a Dutch millionaire to write a psychological study of Van Gogh, talked her way into being a store's improbable fashion buyer in order to live in Norwich for three months, and did supply teaching in absolutely the worst school in Nottingham, replacing teachers dispatched with nervous breakdowns.

Helen wrote her first book in the early sixties to amuse herself when she was ill. Until then her ambition was to be a poet, and she sees her poetry as leading her to fantasy. In both, the unconscious plays an essential role. "You must have the faith to let an idea lie, even for years, until the right moment – which you'll recognise – to start a book. I never know where a story is going: about a third of the way through I suddenly realise what it's about, and that moment is the best thing there is!" The discovery process continues: fantasy or farce, long after a book is written she begins to see its meaning, and now realises that some of her early books were quite deep.

Television has played an important part in her career, not just by increasing her audience but by shaping her stories. Many have been on *Jackanory*, and she has frequently written books in tandem with the screenplays of such enormously popular serials as *Lizzie Dripping*, *The Secret World of Polly Flint*, *The Haunted School* or *Moondial*. "My plots wandered less when I had to write alongside a TV serial."

For many readers, Helen Cresswell's name means not fantasy but *The Bagthorpes*, that hilarious family of eccentrics. She wrote the first of the Saga, *Ordinary Jack* (published 1977) to cheer herself up after a year in which she had lost both her parents and written the complex *The Winter of the Birds* (1975). At first, she couldn't believe they were real people, but later saw that they were based partly on her own childhood and partly on her present family.

That family includes Boris, "an archetypal shaggy dog with pudding feet" who turned up in *The Secret World of Polly Flint*, Buddles, a cream Persian cat, and her younger daughter who played Lizzie Dripping's baby brother – a startling discovery for her future boyfriends.

SELECTED TITLES

Lizzie Dripping
(BBC Books), 1973-74

The Piemakers
(Faber), 1976

The Bagthorpe Saga
(Faber), 1977-89

The Secret World of Polly Flint
(Faber), 1982

Moondial
(Faber), 1987

The Watchers
(Viking), 1993

Gillian Cross

Photograph copyright © Katie Vandyck, 1993

Budding writers are usually advised by everyone – including many people in this book – to "write about what you know", meaning what is within your own experience.

Gillian Cross is determinedly against this: it's more rewarding to choose an idea that excites you, and then learn about what you don't know. As a result, each of her books is a surprise.

"After all, fiction is fiction. It doesn't matter what the level of reality is, because a story must find its own level of truth." What is important is that it should *feel* true. She does worry sometimes: for instance, would American readers of *The Great Elephant Chase* have their illusion of truth shattered by some small mistake committed by someone who had never seen the places visited by Tad and Cissie? (No.) Gillian turns to experts for help, and says the response is always marvellous. She researched with American historical societies, and then discovered for herself how an elephant behaves and what its skin feels like.

Writing *Wolf*, she talked to the keepers at London Zoo and grabbed an offer to enter the wolves' enclosure to study them. Before writing *Chartbreak* she had known nothing about the rock music world, but incorporated the song-lyrics which had won her daughter a tee-shirt in a competition when she was thirteen – Elizabeth got a fee and a credit in the book. During *Born of the Sun*, she asked an expert to translate into medieval Spanish for her. Only for the historical novel *The Iron Way* did she pick a subject about which she was already confident.

This is a risky strategy. Readers like to know where they stand with an author, but no one can be sure what Gillian's next book will be like. Will it be a horror frolic for younger ones, like *The Demon Headmaster*, or an older thriller, like *On the Edge;* a serious psychological mystery, like *Roscoe's Leap*, or a bouncy junior-school story, like *The Mintyglo Kid?* All that's certain is that it will possess the energy and suspense of a gripping story.

Gillian Cross has been a storyteller all her life. She was born near Wembley Stadium on Christmas Eve in 1945, and grew up on the edge of London. "My parents kept finding more boxes of books that hadn't been unpacked since they moved in – and as each box was unpacked, I read what was in it, from *Little Women* to *How to Take Your Own Cine Films*." However, she always liked stories the best, and she read them, told them and wrote them (but never finished them) all through her childhood.

She studied English at Oxford, took a year out at twenty-one to marry and have a son – and still got a First Class degree. By the time she was a graduate at Sussex University, she also had a four-month-old Elizabeth (who now works in publishing).

Her husband's ladder of promotion as a further education lecturer meant regular moves, so she did various jobs, like Tufty Club lady, making bread in the village bakery, and MP's assistant – the person who directs people with appalling problems to the right place for help. Five novels brought nothing but oh-so-encouraging letters from publishers, until suddenly, one final heave brought two acceptances at once. In 1979 *The Iron Way* was published.

Now, more than twenty books (and a second son-and-daughter set) later, she lives in Wolston, near Coventry. No doubt reflecting the way she writes by leaping into the unknown, she enjoys orienteering – except that, unlike her novels, she often gets lost.

SELECTED TITLES

The Dark Behind the Curtain
(Oxford), 1982

The Demon Headmaster
(Oxford), 1982

The Mintyglo Kid
(Methuen) 1983

Swimathon!
(Methuen), 1986

Wolf
(Oxford), 1990

The Great Elephant Chase
(Oxford), 1992

John Cunliffe

About forty-five years ago, at home in Colne, Lancashire, John Cunliffe used to listen to an enormously popular radio quiz show called *Have a Go!*, which prided itself on "bringing the people to the people".

At that time John was wondering what to do when he left school. He liked writing and books, but did not seem academic – bullying at his tough grammar school had made it hard to study. He was an only child, brought up by his mother in the household of an uncle and aunt, and there was little money for university. Then one evening on *Have a Go!* a young man enthusiastically described his work as a librarian, and suddenly John knew what he wanted to be.

From 1958, when he was twenty-five, until 1973, he worked in all sorts of librarian's jobs. The young man he'd heard on the radio (who became City Librarian of Edinburgh) hadn't finished changing John's life. Incredibly, they met and became friends, and it was he who later directed John towards a vacancy in Buckinghamshire which eventually led to his having a go at being a regional children's schools librarian – unusual, then, for a man. Which led to actually reading children's books. Which led to trying to write them.

In the early sixties, with a wife and baby son, he spent two years in Belgrade, Yugoslavia, as the British Council Librarian. He came home to "an awful, frustrating" job as education librarian in Newcastle, but escaped to six happy years in Brighton, where lots of contact with children led him to think of teaching. He began his new career in Kendal in 1975, and six years later went to Manchester, to set up a school book scheme. But, he says, returning to teaching as deputy head of a very tough inner city school nearly finished him off: "I really think it would have killed me if I hadn't got out." He got out by turning his attention to computers, and becoming a part-time advisory teacher travelling around to schools. In 1988 he gave up even this to become a full-time writer.

It had all begun thirty years ago, one night when his wife couldn't sleep and he told her a story about Farmer Barnes. He wrote two more like it, and had three rejections. But Philippa Pearce – a great publishing editor as well as a great children's author – heard him telling warm-up stories for her talk at a library, and asked to see some. She published *Farmer Barnes Buys a Pig* in 1964.

Picture books, stories, rhymes and poems followed regularly and successfully, but without selling enough for him to give up work. Then in his first teaching job at Kendal, hearing that the BBC were looking for new authors and a producer for *Play School*, he had a go at both. He didn't get the producer's job – but was asked to come back. It's a classic "boo-hurrah story", John says: they were looking for a new series set in the countryside, he suggested a rural postman as the linking character – and Postman Pat was off on his rounds.

Books and fame gradually followed, and Pat became the universal postman. Rosie and Jim, in which John appeared as himself, may, he thinks, outdo even Pat, but he was amazed to discover how many long and tedious hours go into a few minutes of film – filming proved less glamorous than he'd ever imagined!

A friendly soul, he still has his Lancashire accent, but now lives contentedly in a small country town on the edge of the moors near Leeds. Perhaps because he always did have a go, his whole life has turned into a boo-hurrah story.

SELECTED TITLES

Farmer Barnes stories
(André Deutsch
Children's Books),
from 1964

Riddles, Rhymes and Rigmaroles
(André Deutsch
Children's Books), 1971

Giant Kippernose and Other Stories
(André Deutsch
Children's Books), 1972

Postman Pat series
(André Deutsch
Children's Books),
from 1981

Standing on a Strawberry
(André Deutsch
Children's Books), 1987

Rosie and Jim series
(André Deutsch
Children's Books),
from 1991

Roald Dahl

When Roald Dahl died in 1990, he was mourned all over the world – in China, for instance, the first print-run of *Charlie and the Chocolate Factory* was two million, probably the biggest ever for any book. He had been translated into thirty-seven languages, he had become a familiar figure – extremely tall but stooping, and elegantly dishevelled – to children everywhere, and he had become very rich.

Dahl led a life as extreme in its tragedy, excitement and triumphs as any of the sharply twisted stories with which he thrilled adults, or the mischievous fantasies that captured children. Some critics even see a streak of personal cruelty in his work. Certainly his own accounts of his younger life, *Boy* and *Going Solo*, are as vivid as any fiction.

He was born in Llandaff, Cardiff, in 1916; his family was Norwegian, and he spent his boyhood summer holidays in Norway. The first of the tragedies that were to scar his soul happened when Roald was three: a much-loved sister died at the age of eight, followed a few weeks later by his father, leaving his mother to bring up five children alone. He went to a famous public school, Repton: schoolmates still remember his rebellious resentment of any injustice, and he himself never forgot his appalled anger at the savage caning that was allowed in those days.

At eighteen he started work for Shell in Dar-es-Salaam in Tanganyika (now Tanzania); when war broke out he joined the RAF in Kenya, and flew a Hurricane as one of a tiny number of fighter pilots in desperate campaigns over Syria and Greece. A crash in the Western Desert in 1941 sent him home with injuries that required repeated operations ever after, but it led to his becoming Assistant Air Attaché in

Washington and a wonderfully debonair life with presidents, diplomats and stars.

In all these years it had never occurred to him to write. Then, in Washington, C.S. Forester interviewed him about his experiences – Forester, author of the *Hornblower* adventures, was a patriot with distinguished connections and America had not yet joined the war. Roald offered to write his own notes for Forester and "got a bit carried away". Forester wrote back to him, "Did you know you were a writer?", and a famous American magazine, the *Saturday Evening Post*, printed his piece unchanged. "I lost most of that first *Post* fee playing poker with Senator Harry Truman – I've always been a great gambling man." Truman later became US President, and Dahl wrote fabulously well-paid short stories.

He was renowned as a perfectionist. One short story could take six months, the first page a month. *James and the Giant Peach* was published in 1961, the first of what he called his *real* stories, and written with the same fanatical care.

But tragedy still lurked. In 1953 Roald had married a beautiful actress, Patricia Neal (later an Oscar-winner in *Hud* with Paul Newman); their second baby, Theo, suffered severe head injuries in a New York street accident, leading Roald to help design the Wade-Dahl-Till valve to drain fluid from the brain. The same resourceful courage led him to relentlessly nurse and bully Pat back to eventual recovery from a catastrophic brain haemorrhage, but was useless against the grief of his eldest daughter's death from measles at eight – the same age as his sister.

But there were three other daughters (Tessa also writes for children), and in his last years, when he and Pat parted, he married her best friend. He lived on contentedly in the Chilterns, near Great Missenden, in his warren of a Georgian house, enjoying his own controversial pugnacity and the adoration of his fans.

SELECTED TITLES

Charlie and the Chocolate Factory (Allen & Unwin), 1967

Fantastic Mr Fox (Allen & Unwin), 1970

The BFG (Cape), 1982

Boy and *Going Solo* (Cape), 1984 and 1986

Minpins (Cape), 1991

My Year (Cape), 1993

Paula Danziger

Photograph copyright © Katie Vandyck, 1993

That low, husky American voice, the mischievously innocent smile and comfortable figure would have made Paula Danziger popular with British kids when they saw her on *Going Live*, even if they had not already fallen headlong for the jokes and sympathy in her books.

Boys as well as girls enjoy her, "once they're past the girl-oriented covers, and realise my books are often anti-establishment and dumb-joke funny. I've got worse with puns, like the grubs in *This Place Has No Atmosphere* being called lunar-ticks." And – wait for it – this is her favourite joke: What's green and hangs from trees? Giraffe snot. . .

But beneath this galumphing humour there is seriousness. "A book should tell a good story first, but it's a chance to bear witness, too." She gets little pleasure from remembering her own youth – her first novel, *The Cat Ate My Gymsuit*, is the most autobiographical, recalling a fat little kid who hated gym, with out-of-control feelings and a father who yelled a lot.

A child in a class once asked her if she really did hate her father when growing up. "I nodded, and she just went 'Aaahh' – one big sigh – and I wanted to cry for her. I did the adult thing, and said that my parents came from *their* background and had problems with their parents, too, and the sadness is that they really did care. But I don't want to say to kids, 'It's going to be all right and some day you'll love this person', because in reality you may not."

She was born in the American capital, Washington DC, but lived mainly in New Jersey. She was a teacher – needless to say, an effective but unconventional one. The teacher in *Gymsuit*, written in 1970 during the

Vietnam war, is fired for refusing to take the oath of political allegiance. That year Paula, too, left teaching after a battle against the effects of a nightmare car accident. A police car rammed hers from behind at a stop sign – only a whiplash neck injury, but as her mother was driving her to hospital a drunk driver hit them and Paula smashed the windscreen. One of the most frightening results of her injuries was that she had a dreadful struggle to read and write.

Conquering this gave her an understanding of people with brain problems, and she took a Master's degree in reading, involving remedial teaching and literature for adolescents. A graduate assistant with an urban programme in Newark dealing with issues like civil rights, a college counsellor for many years, and organiser of programmes for people with reading problems – all these roles came together when she became a full-time writer.

Now Paula has one home in New York City, one upstate in the country, and one in London. Her niece and three nephews, her brother's children, play a vital part in her life (she phones them from wherever she is) and in her writing. She's addicted to making up stories about people: she'll ask to take photos of someone with, say, fabulously weird hair, and sticks their picture on her fridge until a story takes shape.

But where do those titles come from? Like, *You Can't Eat Your Chicken Pox, Amber Brown* – "Oh, I once knew a little boy who (chuckle) actually did that" – or *Remember Me To Harold Square*, whose English sequel might have featured his cousin Lester but is actually *Thames Doesn't Rhyme With James* – "Well, it sometimes does in America, but, I don't know, I guess my brain is just *warped!*"

SELECTED TITLES

Can You Sue Your Parents For Malpractice? (Heinemann), 1986

Everyone Else's Parents Said Yes! (Heinemann), 1989

Earth To Matthew (Heinemann), 1991

There's a Bat in Bunk Five (Heinemann), 1992

The Divorce Express (Heinemann), 1992

Amber Brown is Not a Crayon (Heinemann), 1993

Anne Fine

One reason Anne Fine writes for children is because she knows that, as a child, "books meant everything, more than everything" to her – she actually cannot remember a time when she couldn't read. When her sister was six and Anne was three, their mother had triplets – three more girls! – which was even rarer in 1950 than now, and more or less out of pity she was allowed to send Anne off to school two years earlier than usual.

Perhaps the spell words can still cast on her began then (*silver; watch; captain; frangipani*), but she was about twelve before she had the idea that she might herself one day write books. Her Granny, without knowing it, was always demonstrating the art of storytelling: on each visit she gloriously embellished any little incident with dialogue and emotional developments, more with every telling throughout the day, so that by the time Anne's father came home at night he would hear a wonderfully crafted, polished story – which was wasted on someone like him who fretted that it wasn't *true*.

His job as an electrical engineer moved the family around. Anne was born in Leicester, lived a while in Hampshire, and spent her secondary school life in Northampton. At Warwick University, where she studied politics and history (and found them boring), she met a clever and restless philosopher, and after they married she followed him all round Britain, America and Canada – wherever he decided to go with his research grants and university posts.

She found writing increasingly difficult as an outsider in a foreign culture: "I have to *know* how my characters would have grown up." After they had moved house seventeen times they agreed she couldn't stand any more, and he stayed in California while she went back to Edinburgh with their two daughters.

Now, if left to herself, she would have been happy to settle for no change in anything – even eating the same food and wearing the same clothes every day – but there was one more move to come. When the girls had gone to university, she and her new partner, a botanist who tries to put smugglers out of business by commercially breeding rare and threatened orchids, went to live in the dales of County Durham.

Reversing the usual order, Anne Fine began with a "young adult" audience and progressed to younger books; now she writes adult novels, short stories for new readers, and novels for the tens and over, all of which receive critical acclaim – in one year, 1990, she won the Guardian Award and the Carnegie Medal (*Goggle-Eyes*), the Smarties Prize (*Bill's New Frock*), and was cited Children's Author of the Year.

Her first book, *The Summer-House Loon* in 1978, tied for third place in a competition for unpublished writers; seven years before, it had been rejected by two publishers, and had since lain forgotten under a bed. Publication set her free, and she has written ever since. Although it is one of her sunniest books, she was ill with depression when she wrote it, whereas her later work, although always compassionate and witty – when not downright farcical – often has a black edge to it.

Despite all the humour ("I've got a file of stolen jokes"), adults sometimes worry about the powerful themes and emotions in her stories – cracked marriages, zoos, old age, nuclear power, gut-spilling rage. . . "In fact, I'm rather protective about young readers who still have to grow in certain ways, to gain a sense of control over their own lives. But perhaps these critics think children have no emotions? Or false emotions?"

SELECTED TITLES

Madame Doubtfire
(Hamish Hamilton), 1987

Crummy Mummy and Me
(André Deutsch
Children's Books), 1988

*The Angel of Nitshill
Road*
(Methuen), 1989

*A Sudden Puff of
Glittering Smoke*
(Genie Trilogy)
(Piccadilly Press), 1989

Book of the Banshee
(Hamish Hamilton), 1991

Flour Babies
(Hamish Hamilton), 1992

AUTHOR

Michael Foreman

Nobody could describe Michael Foreman's childhood better than he does himself in *War Boy*, a picture-storybook for all ages of how he grew up in the seaside village of Pakefield, outside Lowestoft in Suffolk.

He was born the year before the Second World War broke out, and an incendiary bomb dropped through his ceiling when he was three. He thinks his luck may have begun then; at any rate, it makes him feel each day is precious, which may be why he "works all day, every day", drawing and painting when he can, writing when he can't – on planes or waiting for people.

His father had died a month before he was born, but because so many other dads were away in the war he didn't feel unusual. One of the houses on his paper-round turned out to belong to an influential teacher known throughout the art world, who arranged for Michael to join a Saturday morning class and, when he was thirteen, asked his Head (Michael Duane, an influential teacher known throughout the *school* world!) if he could attend Lowestoft Art School two afternoons a week.

He left his secondary modern school (where "non-academic" children used to be sent) at fifteen with no O levels, and did the full four-year Painting course, followed by a year at St Martin's School of Art in London. He married, and, to find work in the year before continuing at the Royal College, began illustrating his first books when he was only twenty-one, in particular his own *The General*, an anti-war story for which his wife wrote the text.

There were no more books for five years while Michael formed a design group and became an art editor on British and American magazines. But from 1967 he has been one of our most prolific and sought-after artists. At first the moral themes of his work caused consternation ("communist tracts" said some American reviewers), but *Dinosaurs and all that Rubbish* (1972) is recognised as a landmark in picture-book publishing, and the forerunners of many awards began to flow in.

A scholarship from the Royal College had sent him to America, and since then he has travelled constantly – some say obsessionally – all over the world. Outside children's books, he is honoured as a travel artist, and his children's pictures gain unique atmosphere from his knowledge of faraway places like India or Australia, as well as his need to go and see nearby ones, such as Alderley Edge for Alan Garner's books.

When he's travelling he never takes anything to read, only his current notebook. "Train journeys are great for daydreaming. Delayed flights are good times for people-watching, and the long limbo hours of night flight ... are rare opportunities for the brain to float, unfettered and de-ranged, into the soup of ideas." But his roots are sturdy. He and his second wife live with their three sons partly in Fulham, London, and partly in St Ives, Cornwall – the glorious Cornwall he has painted in many of his books.

He keeps two or three works in progress, so an idea can simmer for a while, or he can dodge a temporary block. Although he must have produced around a hundred books, he is in such demand that he must also have turned as many away. Books should tell you something, he says, they should do more than occupy a space prettily – after thirty-five years, works like *One World* or *The Boy Who Sailed With Columbus*, or *War Game* (which won the 1993 Smarties Prize) show his moral passion is undimmed.

SELECTED TITLES

War and Peas
(Hamish Hamilton), 1974

City of Gold, by Peter Dickinson
(Gollancz), 1980

A Child's Garden of Verses, by Robert Louis Stevenson
(Gollancz), 1985

War Boy
(Pavilion), 1989

Michael Foreman's World of Fairy Tales
(Pavilion), 1990

Jack's Fantastic Voyage
(Andersen), 1992

AUTHOR • ILLUSTRATOR

Susanna Gretz

Susanna Gretz thinks her Teddybears take themselves rather seriously (but, of course, that's why they're funny), while Roger is a pig who wildly misbehaves. There are times when taking her own advice to young artists, to enter right into the little world they're creating, means that "I feel as if I'm *living* with these critters!"

Susanna in fact commits herself wholeheartedly to an unexpected range of interests. She was born in New York City, and grew up in neighbouring New Jersey. Although she had always drawn when she was little, she dropped it for a degree in English and American literature at Smith, a famously academic women's college in Massachusetts – why, she can't imagine now, because Smith's reputation for art was high. But in those days she was set to be A Poet.

After a year in a dead-end secretarial job, she joined the Red Cross (nothing medical!), which involved all sorts of artwork and a chance to travel. She spent two years in Virginia, followed by two in Germany, where she was able to save enough money for a two-year course at a German art school, encouraged by the boyfriend she was to marry.

A visit to London with a portfolio of Teddybear prototypes brought a publishing offer, and the start of a long partnership with her editor, Alison Sage, who collaborated with her on many of the Teddybear texts – they suspected the bears were nearing the end at last when they found themselves choking with laughter at suggestions for more and more unsuitable things for them to say.

Susanna and her husband moved to England for a year, and then to Algeria, where for three years he was an industrial designer for the steel industry. The impact of Algerian life on her, raising all sorts of questions about different cultures and customs, sent her back to Germany for a sociology degree.

She parted from her husband, and in 1979 returned to Britain: she had work contacts here and some friends, and her previous stay in the famously rebellious year of 1968-69 had made her think it was an exciting place. She still thinks that, and she's still here, living with her new partner near White City in west London.

In Germany she had often worked in youth clubs, and it was her voluntary art workshops, twice a week with the youngest teens in a Notting Hill club, that inspired her to keep her studies going. Why were the older boys so hostile to the whole idea of art? She started looking at the attitude to it in primary schools this century – a kind of "sociology of education", and ended with a Master's degree at the Institute of Education.

And, through all this, there were her own books. She even used to work "nerve-wrackingly" on more than one at a time, until she ended up at an osteopath's with a stiff neck. Although she has successfully illustrated other writers (like John Agard), her own characters inevitably mean more to her – the prize-winning Roger or the volatile friendship of Frog, Duck and Rabbit. Translated into nine languages, from Frisian to Afrikaans, as animals they lack all restrictions of race or nationality while still teasingly portraying human silliness – hopefully not a cop-out, says Susanna, but a liberating freedom for her and her readers.

Her video on how a book is made has become a groundrock classic. She enjoyed her conventional author-visits to schools, but after ten years they began to feel stale, so she has developed her vigorous workshop projects of a full day or more with a class – "And, no, I *don't* steal their ideas!"

SELECTED TITLES

It's Your Turn, Roger! (series) (The Bodley Head), 1985

Bedtime Bears series (Hippo), 1990

Frog, Duck and Rabbit series (Methuen), 1991

Crocodile books (Methuen), 1993

Monster Monday (BBC Books), 1994

Video - *Roger's Book: How a Book is Made* (Book Trust), 1989-1990

AUTHOR • ILLUSTRATOR

Jane Hissey

"**I** can't count how many hours of my life I've spent drawing," says Jane Hissey. "I know *Jolly Snow* took 800 hours – and that's not a very elaborate book." Jane's career is often made to sound like a magical tale of discovery and success, but she began working on books when her daughter Alison was born, which represents "ten years of solid work – scarcely a fairy story!"

Until then, book illustration had never entered Jane's mind: she assumed that her combination of A level art, zoology and botany would point her towards something like medical illustration. Born and brought up in Norwich, she had a foundation year at Great Yarmouth Art College, before taking a design and illustration course at Brighton College of Art (chosen because she imagined seaside Brighton would be like Yarmouth).

Without her fully realising it then, Brighton cast two permanent influences over her life. First, her discovery of the pencil-crayon medium (exactly the same as the enticing Caran d'Ache rainbows children use) gave her new confidence in her abilities, and although the building up in layers of its effect is so time-consuming, it does allow her to stop-and-start – invaluable when she's trying to run a home. Second, among Brighton's teachers were brilliant illustrators like John Vernon Lord and Raymond Briggs, who had personal and *active* knowledge of children's books.

She met her future husband, himself a graphic designer, whose understanding but avoidance of long-term projects like Jane's has turned their marriage into fine teamwork. They remained beside the sea, and Jane taught art in a sixth-form college in Worthing for five years, until the birth of Owen, who's now thirteen. (Eventually they did desert the seaside; today they live near Ashdown Forest in East Sussex.)

At home with her baby, Jane drew for pleasure, building a portfolio based on the principle, "Draw what's to hand." What was to hand was a bear a friend had made for Owen. Soon her pictures were being displayed among the furniture of The General Trading Company, and she was doing commissioned portraits of customers' beloved teddies. When a friend sent Jane's work to a greetings card company, she moved into print.

If any fairy godmothers were waving wands, this was the moment. An editor from publishers Hutchinson saw her cards, and rang to suggest she try a children's book.

Jane Hissey would have been astonished to be told her stories were to be almost as popular as her pictures; ironically, it was television, a visual medium, that turned 1992 into a wholly writing year, because she had to provide four extra stories – their future pictures only in her mind – for her animated series.

Old Bear and Alison were born together, but Old Bear is more famous – he's treasured in a dozen countries – and is actually as old as her mum, being Jane's childhood teddy. Other characters come from among the children's toys, although "characters" is perhaps the wrong word, because it is their *texture* as much as their character that prompts the inclusion of, for instance, Jolly Tall or Zebra.

"I set them up as a still-life indoors, even if it's an 'outdoor' picnic. One drawing can take a week of painstaking labour, a whole book a year, so I couldn't draw from living models! Before Ralph (who's three) was born, I could have worked while the children were at school, but I found I had come to prefer the evenings – at certain stages the work is semi-mechanical, and it's quite soothing to be absorbed in it at the end of the day, not thinking of anything else."

SELECTED TITLES

Old Bear books
(Hutchinson), from 1986

Little Bear books
(Hutchinson), 1989-90

Jolly Tall
(Hutchinson), 1990

*The Jane Hissey
Collection*
(Hutchinson), 1990

Jolly Snow
(Hutchinson), 1991

Russell Hoban

Photograph copyright © Tana Hoban, 1991

He is a short man and apparently shy, but those anxious eyes behind their glasses conceal one of the most powerful blends of intellect and imagination in the world of books. To talk to Russell Hoban can be as amusing, comforting or puzzling as to read him.

Russell was born in rural Pennsylvania, in America, and from the age of five his talent for drawing led everyone to take it for granted that he'd be an artist. At sixteen he went for two years to art school in Philadelphia, before being swept into the Second World War as an infantryman (he won a Bronze Star) and into a very young marriage.

After the war he was an illustrator for magazines and advertising, a storyboard artist in films, and a television art director. Then he settled down (he thought) to being a freelance illustrator, working at home in Connecticut. But in 1959 he began to write and illustrate his own non-fiction children's books, and gradually the two careers overlapped.

His first story book, *Bedtime for Frances*, had pictures by Garth Williams, but his next, in 1961, was illustrated by his wife Lillian. It was the perfect match, and began a ten-year partnership that produced some of the most loved of all small children's books, particularly the continuing story of Frances, the little badger. It dawned that he was a writer rather than an illustrator; to earn a living – he now had a son and three daughters – he returned to work in advertising as a copywriter, writing his books at night.

The climax of this period was his first long novel, *The Mouse and His Child*, published in 1967 after four years of thought and work. Exciting and scary, mysterious and sad, it has something to say to everyone, grown-up or ten years old, and it soon joined the ranks of immortal classics. Russell had seen the original mouse and child under a friend's Christmas tree; he still has it, and the mouse still turns round and round, swinging his baby into the air in their own world of clockwork immortality.

At this point his life changed. He became a full-time writer, restless to tackle demanding fiction; he had to deal with ill-health; and the family moved to London, a place where he felt mentally at home. "As far back as I can remember, all my favourite writers have been English or Irish." But his marriage broke up. Lillian and the children were never at home here, and eventually returned to America – the pain he felt at the loss of his children is reflected in the themes of his later adult novels.

While garlanded for the originality of those novels, he has continued to write a stream of imaginative frolics for young children: *How Tom Beat Captain Najork and His Hired Sportsmen* (which won the Whitbread Award), *The Dancing Tigers* or the *Jim Hedgehog* stories – fifty-seven so far. They are a relaxation but also, he says, rather like poetry. "The work might only take a day or a week, but it's very concentrated and intense."

Russell has lived in Fulham, London, for twenty-one years now, with his second family – Gundula, who came to England from Germany as a bookseller, and three more sons, Jake, Ben and Wieland (check them out in *They Came From Aargh!* and *The Great Fruit Gum Robbery*).

Here, he says, he found himself. "People say that every artist has a particular theme which he goes through over and over again, and I suppose mine has to do with placing the self – finding a place – and in one way or another most of my characters in my books go through it."

SELECTED TITLES

The Mouse and His Child (Faber), 1969

Dinner at Alberta's (Cape), 1977

The Twenty-Elephant Restaurant (Cape), 1980

The Marzipan Pig (Cape), 1986

Jim Hedgehog and the Lonesome Tower (Hamish Hamilton), 1990

Court of the Winged Serpent (Cape), 1994

Photograph by Paul Cox

Shirley Hughes

If Lucy and Tom had been able to grow older like real children, they would now be in their thirties. But they are still in a book, tousle-haired and bouncy, eager to explore the world once more with each generation of toddlers.

Shirley Hughes, the young mum who drew them, was certainly real and she now has three grandchildren. A stately figure, warm and talkative, she is one of the most energetic and influential people in the world of children's books. Few illustrators have done more, through technical knowledge of page-layouts, artistic genius and a loving interest in young people, to help children unravel the mystery of reading. And enjoy it.

She didn't foresee this when she was young. She wanted to be a stage designer. And she did study costume design, which proved useful for the historical dress in tales like *Peter Pan and Wendy* and *The Secret Garden* – and for making her own clothes.

She was born and grew up in West Kirkby, near Liverpool. She was a teenager during the war, and remembers how they watched world-shattering events in the midst of everyday boredom. They saw the Liverpool docks in flames every night, and enjoyed the excitement of American GI soldiers, "unbelievable people arriving from nowhere," but food was dull and no one could go anywhere. So she and her two sisters continued to draw, write stories and perform plays for years longer than children might today.

Shirley went to Liverpool School of Art, and briefly painted sets and pinned costumes for Birmingham Repertory Theatre. Although this got rid of any notions of working in the theatre, it helped her understand the link between the stage – lighting, grouping, gestures – and book illustration. This later evolved into a link with film techniques, like the "split-page" in *Alfie Gets In First*, which allows you to see inside and outside Alfie's house at the same time.

She returned to drawing, and studied for three years at the Ruskin School, Oxford. Unlike subsequent generations of students, she endured the discipline of anatomy examinations and life drawing from a model, but was grateful later; on the other hand, illustration courses didn't exist then, and she learnt the art herself. She married an architect, and says he taught her the lessons in perspective, "shadows and things", that art school missed.

When she was looking for work in the 1950s, pony books were the rage. But editors recognised her ability to draw real kids, not the prim stereotypes of the time, and switched her to adventures with children romping around Scottish moors. Her line drawings illustrated dozens of books, by unknown writers and famous ones, until true success arrived in 1968, when Dorothy Edwards asked her to re-illustrate her popular *Naughty Little Sister* stories.

The family moved to a quiet road in Notting Hill, London, amid the streets you glimpse so often in her books. As her children grew up – two sons, one in journalism and the other in medical research, and a daughter who is herself an artist married to an artist – she found the energy and time to experiment. First, diffidently, with colour, which she builds up layer on layer towards the foreground, giving her pictures depth "like opening up a stage". Then, boldly, with the placing of words and pictures. Sometimes there are no words; sometimes people talk in bubbles; sometimes the action moves in frames, like a film. Each book pushes through another design barrier.

With well over 200 books behind her, she and her sketchbook are never idle. "I collect faces as other people might collect stamps."

SELECTED TITLES

Dogger
(The Bodley Head), 1977

Up and Up
(The Bodley Head), 1979

Alfie books
(The Bodley Head), 1982-3

Chips and Jessie books
(The Bodley Head), 1985

The Snow Lady
(Walker), 1990

Stories by Firelight
(The Bodley Head), 1993

AUTHOR • ILLUSTRATOR

Ted Hughes

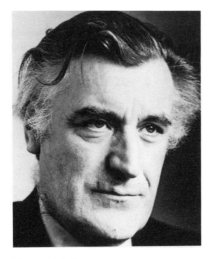

Photograph by Jane Brown

Ben Jonson in 1619 was our first official Poet Laureate. In 1984, Edward James Hughes – never known as anything but Ted – became our latest: he earns £70 a year and a case of wine.

Ted remembers as a boy snatching up mice scattered by the threshing machines at harvest time, until he had forty in his coat lining: for him, capturing animals is like capturing, writing, a poem. He's a sinewy poet who writes in very physical imagery.

He has observed animals closely and with passion all his life, and they provide him with metaphors about humans' inner drives and fears. This is particularly clear in the linked poems of *What is the Truth?*. God's Son puts this question to different villagers and they each try to answer by singing about their own choice from all the animals and birds of the countryside.

Ted Hughes was born in 1930, in the Pennine village of Mytholmroyd, and reckons that the West Yorkshire dialect is really what he writes. He had an elder sister and brother – "dazzling stars" who, in one way, gave him his competitive streak, but also, he says, urged and coaxed him into everything he is now. Like a retriever, he used to accompany his brother hunting and shooting on the hillsides and moors.

When he was eight they moved, and Ted went to Mexborough Grammar School where he led two separate lives: one with his town friends, sons of colliers and railwaymen, and one in his "bolthole", a local farm and estate. Discovering D. H. Lawrence, he remembers, was like reading his own autobiography. Around fifteen Ted's attitude to animals changed, and he began to see them from their point of view. And he began to write poems, although not, curiously, about animals.

He did his National Service as a wireless mechanic in the RAF (and at nineteen wrote the earliest poem in his first book), and went on to Cambridge University to study English. Although, for him, "Eng Lit" became a deadening prison from which he escaped into Archaeology and Anthropology, and although for two years afterwards he "kicked around" – teacher, rose-gardener, nightwatchman, scriptwriter – all through this time he continued writing. At Cambridge his efforts had felt confused and unfocused, but within six months of graduating he finished his "Jaguar" pieces and "Wind", and by 1956, when he married, he'd already written all but a few of the forty poems in his adult collection, *The Hawk in the Rain*. It was published in 1957 to instant acclaim.

He had married a then-unknown American poet, Sylvia Plath; they had a son and a daughter, Frieda, who now writes children's books herself. Sylvia suffered from a depressive illness and committed suicide in 1963, but throughout their brief marriage they fired each other to write intensely, and her work came to be much studied and revered.

In 1970 Ted married again, and now lives in a rambling old house in the countryside near Okehampton. From 1972 he became committed to the Arvon Foundation, established by two fellow poets, whose summer schools have helped hundreds of adult new writers. He is not just a poet but a natural teacher, who has worked tirelessly to encourage anyone, young or old, to learn not "How to write" but "How to try to say what you really mean".

He has always written for children – stories like *The Iron Man* and *How The Whale Became*, plays like *The Coming of the Kings*, and many poetry collections, lighthearted and serious. The care and tenderness with which he campaigns and writes for young people make him much more their Poet Laureate than any Royal Person's.

SELECTED TITLES

How the Whale Became
(Faber), 1963

The Iron Man
(Faber), 1968

What is the Truth?
(Faber), 1984

Ffangs the Vampire Bat and the Kiss of Truth
(Faber), 1986

Tales of the Early World
(Faber), 1988

The Iron Woman
(Faber), 1993

Pat Hutchins

There's a down-to-earthness about Pat Hutchins's voice and sense of humour which reminds you that she comes from a big Yorkshire family. She was born halfway through the war in the village of Scorton, the sixth of seven children; they had little money but a Mum who believed in children doing what they wanted.

All Pat wanted was to draw. When collecting paraffin from a neighbouring elderly couple, retired teachers, she showed them what she could do by drawing on an old chocolate-bar wrapper. Mr and Mrs Bruce became loving supporters, who lived long enough to see Pat's success, to have *Changes* dedicated to them – and to see their portraits in *The Wind Blew*.

She won a scholarship to Darlington Art School when she was sixteen. "I was happy to go. Somehow in Yorkshire people think you're a bit weird if you like to draw and go off for long walks on your own. I was beginning to feel I was a bit of a freak." She went on to specialise in illustration at Leeds College of Art, before going to London and trying to get published – without success.

Instead she became an assistant art director with J. Walter Thomson, a famous advertising agency, where she met her husband Laurence, a film director and artist. He was later to illustrate her longer books, chaotically funny stories like *Follow That Bus!* and *The Mona Lisa Mystery* – "I couldn't do the sort of cartoony drawings those books needed." When, a week after they married, Laurence was sent to the New York branch, Pat decided to try her luck with American publishers.

When she offered an idea for a long book about

farmyard noises, there was just *one line* the editor liked: "This is the fox. He never makes a noise." Prompted to write around that, Pat took the editor literally and began to view her story like a silent film (or a pantomime) where the audience can see what's happening but the heroine can't. It took a year of work, of abandoning text and any ideas of glorious technicolor, to end up with the thirty-two words and classic three-colour illustrations of that immortal picture book, *Rosie's Walk.*

This was 1968. Pat and Laurence returned to London and had two sons, Morgan and Sam who, as they grew up, inspired and starred in many of Pat's books. After *Follow That Bus!* more and more of Morgan's mates turned up to ask if they could be in the next one, so *The Mona Lisa Mystery* has an even larger cast. When *The House That Sailed Away* was on *Jackanory*, Grandma, Pat's mum, was working as a tea-lady in a hospital and got a terrible teasing about her curlers and champagne.

Laurence's drawings show a recognisable Camden Town, in north London, not too far from the Hutchins' home in Hampstead. Laurence, mad about model steam trains, has a track in the garden, while indoors is the kind of clutter that comes when two people love collecting old things and can't throw anything away – and Pat hoards odd items for reference when she's drawing. Today Morgan is a film director himself, and "baby" Sam is a chef.

When sent away to write that first story Pat was terrified, but she now thinks of herself as a writer rather than an artist, and has even written plays for the theatre. "I think it's because I don't know anything about writing. My English is appalling, but because I don't know it's appalling I just get on with it and enjoy it."

SELECTED TITLES

Titch
(The Bodley Head), 1971

Goodnight, Owl!
(The Bodley Head), 1973

The Very Worst Monster
(The Bodley Head), 1985

Rats!
(The Bodley Head), 1989

Which Witch is Which?
(Julia MacRae), 1990

My Best Friend
(Julia MacRae), 1993

AUTHOR • ILLUSTRATOR

Photograph by Susan Greenhill

Mick Inkpen

A writer and artist called Inkpen? Although he's been told his name actually meant "Hillhill" for deaf or disbelieving Saxons, it *might* have conjured the quirk of fate that changed the direction of Mick Inkpen's life.

When he took a year off between school and starting an English degree at Cambridge University, his A level art landed him a temporary job in the graphic design studio of a friend, Nick Butterworth, who had been at the same grammar school about seven years earlier. Temporary turned into permanent, and eventually the Mick-Nick partnership was to produce that endearing clown, Jasper the kitten, and primary school classics like *The Nativity Play*.

Mick Inkpen was born a couple of days before Christmas 1952 in Romford, on the eastern edge of London, and lived there all his life until recently. Then the snowballing success of his own picture books – which began with *One Bear at Bedtime*, gathered pace with the *The Blue Balloon*'s unfolding surprise, rolled through prize-winners *Threadbare* and *Penguin Small* and into the unstoppable *Kipper* books – allowed him to move to a little village in the "Constable country" of the Stour valley near Colchester.

He half regrets missing Cambridge ("it would have been a rich, broadening experience") and admits he'd encourage his own kids not to do the same, but feels lucky to end up with both writing and art. The design studio "was an excellent grounding – a kind of informal apprenticeship where I learned as much about dealing with stroppy printers and difficult clients as about the finer points of typography."

Among his first commissions were designing bra packs for The Lovable Company and struggling to find cartoon ideas to brighten up articles on insurance. It sounds a giggle, but the layers of committee decisions which such artists must work through are always frustrating. And, says Mick, "design is not a high priority of British companies." Come to think of it, it *was* a giggle: they all larked around the studio so much that Mick thought it was perhaps time for him to go freelance and *work*.

It was twelve years before he moved into the world of children's books, when his own children were toddlers – Simon is now thirteen, Chloë eleven. He was not writing specifically for them, but they helped him understand what makes real children tick. He and Nick Butterworth teamed up to produce around thirty titles, and they had a brief, fraught period with *Rub-A-Dub-Tub* on TV-AM in its fragile early days, when both budgets and nerves were strung out.

For some years Mick, like Anthony Browne and Babette Cole, designed greetings cards for Gordon Fraser; such one-off designs allowed him to experiment with techniques, and ideas for books sometimes evolved from them. In 1986, Butterworth set off to test himself in television and Inkpen made his first conscious decision to go for a solo career as "A Children's Author", a formal description he'd regarded up till then as somehow presumptuous. Over-modest: his career was carried to new heights by a soaring *Blue Balloon* – the moment he saw it displayed face-upwards in shops, instead of being buried in a row of thin spines, he knew he had made it! Soon *Penguin Small* was Picture Book of the Year.

Now he has widened his appeal with his Inkpops, rhyming mini pop-ups with a nicely wicked humour, and the beguiling Kipper refused to lie down quietly until he got more stories of his own. Kipper would seem a natural for television fame, although Mick has little time for the mostly stunted animation churned out by TV. Yet who knows what a quirk of fate might have in store?

SELECTED TITLES

The Blue Balloon (Hodder & Stoughton), 1989

Jojo's Revenge (Walker), 1989

Kipper books (Hodder & Stoughton), from 1991

Jasper's Beanstalk, with Nick Butterworth (Hodder & Stoughton), 1992

Penguin Small (Hodder & Stoughton), 1992

Threadbear, (Hodder & Stoughton), 1992

AUTHOR • ILLUSTRATOR

73

Photograph by Mike Laye

Terry Jones

When he was six Terry Jones wrote, "I am hopping to be an actor" – he reckoned he was already a poet, even if not in joined-up writing. Grown-up Terry ("I'm the same person I was when I was six. I've just learnt to cover up things that are embarrassing") has actually been an actor, and has decided he likes writing children's stories better than anything else. He can certainly do it faster than almost anything else.

He was born, a good Welsh Jones, in Colwyn Bay in 1942, but left at five for Claygate, Surrey, going to grammar school in Guildford. His father was a bank clerk who, Terry recalls sadly, would rather have been a carpenter.

He studied English at Oxford, where he spent a lot of his time worrying, some of it designing and writing for the university magazine, and all the rest designing, writing and acting in highly successful revues which went on to the Edinburgh Festival, Stratford and London's West End. Among his theatrical friends, who all found fame of different kinds, were a young singer who was to become the children's writer Adèle Geras, and Michael Palin, who was to become his lifelong friend and collaborator.

When Terry "somehow" became involved in television he put Michael into one of his films on his training course, and together they produced little sketches for *The Frost Report*. They teamed up with Eric Idle and Terry Gilliam for a way-out children's programme called *Do Not Adjust Your Set* ("Well, *we* thought it was funny!"), now remembered as a great mould-breaker. For a while Terry and Michael eagerly wrote anything for anyone; then all four met up again with their Cambridge opposite numbers, John Cleese and Graham Chapman, and by 1969 the crazily surreal

"Monty Python" group had evolved.

He'd always wanted to make films, but as An Actor; now he found himself not only performing but writing and, eventually, directing. There were three gloriously anarchic Python films between 1975 and 1983, which, like the TV shows, immediately gained cult status.

In 1971 he had married Alison, a scientist who, unknown to him then, had been a fellow student. It was when their daughter Sally was five and he had "a free week" that he began his *Fairy Tales* for her, "full of witches, monsters and frightening bits". He wrote one or two a day: publication was not so easy.

He had already written (seriously for once, if not solemnly) a startling new scholar's view of Chaucer's Knight from *The Canterbury Tales*, the blossoming of a near-obsession that had taken root fifteen years earlier at Oxford and has grown ever since, right up to his forthcoming television series on the Crusades. A chance meeting with its editor, who'd become an independent publisher, ended three whole years of rejections for *Fairy Tales*.

After all that, it was a best seller, popular in six languages. It was also the start of his long partnership with artist Michael Foreman, who described the fun he was having with Terry's next book, *The Saga of Erik the Viking*, as "It's like Saturday morning pictures, a cliff hanger in every chapter." This one was for Bill, who had demanded blood and thunder.

Today Terry is an internationally recognised film director, Sally is twenty and Bill seventeen, but the irreverent pleasure in writing for children is still there – four books later, *Fantastic Stories* displayed the invention and energy undimmed. And he is still firing satirical cannon balls against political insanity and wickedness.

Can this be the man who says his greatest literary influence is Rupert Bear? What will he hop for next?

SELECTED TITLES

Fairy Tales
(Pavilion), 1981

The Saga of Erik the Viking
(Pavilion), 1983

Nicobobinus
(Pavilion), 1985

The Curse of the Vampire's Socks and other Doggerel
(Pavilion), 1988

Fantastic Stories
(Pavilion), 1992

AUTHOR

Gene Kemp

Photograph by Exeter Express & Echo

When Gene Kemp's mother named her baby after Gene Stratton Porter (author of *A Girl of the Limberlost*, an American classic), she probably didn't know her real name had been Geneva.

"Geneva Kemp" would seem hilarious to the three little girls who rampage through Grandma's House every week, to play in her wilderness of a garden, full of wildlife and fruit trees, or prepare for an expedition to the beach or the moors. This is the house, between Exeter and Dartmoor, where their mother grew up, and Gene still lives there with one grown-up son and Scroggins, a wicked cat whose sole aim in life is to catch her ten goldfish.

She greatly cherishes her granddaughters' close presence in Exeter. Not far away is the University where she got her English degree, never imagining that in later life it would honour her with a Master of Arts in recognition of her work as a children's writer.

Gene was born in Wigginton, a Midlands village outside Tamworth – her first book, *The Prime of Tamworth Pig* in 1972, grew out of memories of the pigs which families like theirs used to keep, to be turned not into pets but breakfasts and dinners. (Just like Nina Bawden's – see page 16.)

She returned home from university to marry her first husband: with their baby daughter (she also has two sons from her second marriage) she taught in a tiny Devon school while they lived on Dartmoor – a bleak place, she says, that would have finished off *any* faltering marriage.

She was used to teaching, having often helped her older sister who was a teacher – it is typical of Gene that she walked out of her formal training. With three children, they had little money, so she taught full-time in both primary and secondary schools. She has always hated "being stuck", however, and took courses at a teacher-training college in Exmouth "to brighten myself up". Then, after presenting a paper she'd written to one enthusiastic audience, she was offered the position of lecturer herself.

The 1970s were a bright, stimulating era for students and politics, and she gladly joined in the life. This gave her the confidence to enter the world of writing, and she posted off *The Turbulent Term of Tyke Tiler*, which was published in 1977 and immediately won the Carnegie Medal. After that, she decided she could risk going freelance.

Tyke went on winning awards, and has been translated into fourteen languages (those chapter heading jokes pose terrible problems!). The monster brats, cheeky and brave, of Cricklepit School are dear to her – she feels Charlie Lewis is near to herself: "I like the idea of what's going on in people's heads."

Memories of what was going on in her own eight-year-old head prompted *The Well*. She wrote it, "a page an evening of my own life," when her husband was in hospital, remembering the well in their childhood garden, and the sheer power of her young imagination because she believed her brother's stories about what lay beyond the garden wall.

Although she has written for teenagers (*No Place Like*), Gene prefers a middle-school audience. "That's a magical age, before kids become self-regarding." She loves *talking* to children, but maintains she hates writing, hates letters.

She also hates being labelled, hates straitjackets that might stop her experimenting with, say, poetry (the fierce countryside of *The Mink War*) short stories (*Roundabout*), or silly ghosts. But the chirpiness, variety and inventive unruliness of her work is always steadied by tenderness, and the recognition that underdogs have their own dignity.

SELECTED TITLES

Tamworth Pig stories
(Faber), from 1972

The Turbulent Term of Tyke Tiler
(Faber), 1977

Gowie Corby Plays Chicken
(Faber), 1979

Juniper
(Faber), 1986

Just Ferret
(Faber), 1990

Roundabout
(Faber), 1993

Dick King-Smith

Everything, says Dick King-Smith, has turned out dishy. He and his wife Myrle live in a twisty seventeenth-century house in an oatmeal-coloured village near Keynsham, Avon, close to where he was born. Once they had a whole menagerie of dogs, guinea-pigs, ducks and everything else you could think of, but ten (at the last count) visiting grandchildren probably still liven it up. The King-Smiths bought it with the help of a friend at a lucky auction, in the days when they were more or less homeless.

Good luck and good friends rescued Dick and Myrle many a time before he discovered the genius for funny, heart-warming and exciting animal stories that has brought him fame and fortune.

He married Myrle in 1943 when they were both twenty; it was wartime, and she was with Fighter Command while he was in the Grenadier Guards. A romantic story, but savage complications from a wound he received in Italy almost ended it. It took three years to recover, and then they began twenty years of attractive but uncommercial farming which left them with no home, no money and three children. Friends helped out; he tried selling fire-fighting suits; he worked in a boot factory.

Almost despairing, he took a chance when he was nearing fifty and began to train as a teacher, with an education degree from Bristol University. It was a turning-point. He taught for seven years at a primary school near Bath, and began writing for that age-group in the holidays. He was an immediate success. Admittedly, he had already been writing witty verses for magazines like *Punch*, where his *Alphabeasts* had first appeared twenty-five years before they were made into a book in 1990.

Then television's *Rub-a-Dub-Tub*, looking for a rare farmer/teacher/writer combination, found Dick and Dodo, a charmingly exhibitionist little dachshund; later Dick presented *Pob* before he and Dodo went to *Tumbledown Farm*. "I'm a show-off, actually," he says – like Dodo, perhaps. The TV connection and his lifelong knowledge of the countryside allowed him to branch out into books about pets, wildlife and conservation.

He says his first novel, *The Fox Busters*, was as stark as a war report when his editor saw the first draft: no dialogue, no characterisation. She was "a smashing, educating editor", and he learned his lessons quickly. But it is this economy of words (the result, he believes, of a classical education at Marlborough College) that saves his animal heroics from whimsy.

Many people dislike anthropomorphic books – that is, where human characteristics are given to non-human things. But Dick King-Smith shares with Beatrix Potter and Kipling (much-loved writers whom Dick himself read when he was young) an ability to give animals speech and emotions – and remarkable talents! – while keeping them faithful to their animal nature. His affection for his animals is grounded in his farming knowledge. Pigs, for example, such as the endearing and immortal Babe in *The Sheep-Pig*, are indeed the cleverest animals on the farm.

The award-winning *The Sheep-Pig* was Dick's sixth novel, and is still most readers' favourite. But once started, the stories have never stopped and he is now one of our most prolific authors for younger children. Whether about animals or human families, most have a touch of magic and fantasy, and all have an irresistible urge to play around with words and puns. But even at his jokiest, Dick King-Smith stresses the importance of being decent, courteous and loving to one another.

Which perhaps explains his own "luck".

SELECTED TITLES

The Sheep-Pig
(Gollancz), 1983

Harry's Mad
(Gollancz), 1984

The Hodgeheg
(Hamish Hamilton), 1987

Paddy's Pot of Gold
(Viking), 1990

Sophie stories
(Walker), 1991

All Pigs are Beautiful
(Walker), 1993

AUTHOR

Joan Lingard

Once, when Joan Lingard was eleven and fed up with their tatty local library, her mother suggested she write her own book. From that moment she knew that some day, some way, she would be a writer. Now she has written about a dozen books for adults, and twice as many for young people.

Born in Edinburgh, she moved to Belfast when she was two and her father was posted there during the war with the Royal Navy Volunteer Reserve. With an English father and a Scottish mother, and a quaintly relaxed Christian Science upbringing, she always felt something of an outsider. She left school at sixteen, shattered by the death of her mother, to whom she had been very close. Quite untrained, she struggled to teach six-year-olds in a dreadfully run-down school, tried to work in a bank, and finally, at eighteen, returned to Edinburgh to work in a library. She still wanted to be a writer, but never felt able to say so out loud. Then she found herself training properly to be a teacher – definitely *not* an experience she enjoyed.

She wrote her first novel, a "hymn of hate", about that training course. She burnt it, but went on to publish six adult novels. One was about Ulster, and someone suggested she write one for young people about what was happening there. Suddenly she realised that *The Twelfth Day of July* was "just waiting to pop out". She meant to write only one, but found she longed to discover what happened to Protestant Sadie and Catholic Kevin, so she wrote *Across the Barricades*. In the end, the story of their love and exile, the problems of their marriage and the pressures from their faraway families, turned into a quintet which has continued to be read and loved ever since.

"When you write for young people, you lower your bucket into the well of your own childhood and adolescence. That's my framework, and I realise it more and more the older I get." Joan's childhood, her family, and the issues she feels strongly about in today's world, all feed into her books. But not people themselves. "I *create* characters," she says, "but *use* material."

In this way, her father's mother (who ran The Monarch pub in Green Lane, Stoke Newington, and a smallholding in what was then rural Welwyn, where Joan went for holidays) is transported to the Highlands to partly reappear as Maggie's grandmother in the *Maggie* quartet.

More dramatically, in *The Guilty Party* young Josie joins a peaceful protest against a nuclear power station, and with stubborn bravery lands herself in Holloway prison. The novel is a tribute to Jenny, the youngest of Joan's three daughters, who was arrested when she was fifteen for flyposting a Youth CND jumble sale, and ended up at eighteen, after eight more arrests, in Holloway. But we must not think Josie *is* Jenny.

Joan's husband, a Canadian architect, was a very real outsider, a "displaced person" who was shunted as a child from Latvia through various German camps. The touching story of the family in the *Tug of War* trilogy is a tribute to all those like him – but it is still imaginary.

Through such characters Joan Lingard brings life to the themes that weave through all her books, for whatever age: having to put down new roots, throwing away the prejudices everyone inherits, friendship, and, perhaps most important for her, freedom. "We inhabit only one body," she says, "but by reading and by writing we can live in many worlds!"

SELECTED TITLES

Kevin and Sadie quintet
(Hamish Hamilton),
from 1972

Maggie quartet
(Hamish Hamilton), 1974-8

The Gooseberry
(Hamish Hamilton), 1978

The Freedom Machine
(Hamish Hamilton), 1986

Frying as Usual
(Hamish Hamilton), 1988

Rags and Riches
(Hamish Hamilton), 1988

Roger McGough

Roger McGough hides his niceness as well as his jokes behind a straight face, just as his performing voice – throwaway-ordinary, curiously jerky – seems to be trying to hide the playfulness in many of his poems. ("Not a performing voice, it's my own.") Yet a Liverpudlian lilt can't help suggesting a cheeky sense of humour.

His is a versatile talent. A performer and a writer, for adults as well as for children (sometimes with the same poem, just as he can be comic and sad at the same time), a dramatist in film, theatre and television, a Name to speak at international conferences and judge awards, McGough had already found one, very different, stardom while the parents of today's young readers were still teenagers.

His work, like, say, the stories in *The Stowaways,* is full of echoes of his own childhood. He was born in Liverpool and was a small boy during the war. Liverpool in those days was a great port, Britain's gateway to the Atlantic, vital not just militarily but to feed the nation. Roger could lie in bed and listen to the mighty chorus of ships' hooters as they edged their way out to sea to exotic faraway places.

His dad worked on the docks. Literary books were never part of family life, although his mother enjoyed "a good read" and his parents saw education as the way to get on. Roger went to a conventionally solemn grammar school which did little to make him relish literature (except his favourite comics like the *Hotspur*), and he even managed to fail his O level English literature. He studied French and geography (chosen because they were his best A levels) at Hull University (chosen because it wasn't too far away and he liked their scarf), before training to be a teacher.

At Hull, however, he discovered poetry – partly from an inspiring recording of Dylan Thomas's verse play for radio, *Under Milk Wood,* partly through French poets like Rimbaud and Baudelaire, and partly from eventually finding the courage to show his work to the poet Philip Larkin, the university librarian and sub-warden of Roger's hall of residence. He had thought that in order to write contemporary poetry "you had to be travelled and widely-read to put in a lot of classical references", but one night he found himself writing through until dawn. He had discovered himself. He knew that, no matter how he would earn his living, he was a poet.

In the sixties he returned to Liverpool to teach, a new sparkling Liverpool that had become world-famous as the fount of pop culture. He was writing not only poetry, but lyrics and sketches as part of a performing group (it included Michael McCartney, brother of Paul) who became internationally popular as The Scaffold, with hits like "Lily the Pink", and the script for *The Yellow Submarine.* It was a frenzied, always-on-the-road, big-money-soon-gone period.

Plays and verse flowed from him, some of it to reappear later in teenage collections, but it was 1976, following a poetry fellowship at Loughborough University, before he published *Mr Noselighter* specifically for children, relishing a light-hearted fooling around with words inspired by his son Finn. Classic collections like *You Tell Me,* the award-winning *Sky in the Pie* or *Nailing the Shadow* have followed at regular intervals.

Finn and Tom are grown up now, Roger is remarried and lives in Barnes, between a duck pond and the Thames, with Matthew, who's seven, and Isabel, three. Two new inspirations, yes, but Roger McGough's special qualities have always prevented the adult world from having sole rights.

SELECTED TITLES

Strictly Private (ed)
(Viking), 1981

The Great Smile Robbery
(Viking), 1984

An Imaginary Menagerie
(Viking), 1988

Pillow Talk
(Viking), 1990

You at the Back
(selected poems)
(Cape), 1991

My Dad's a Fireater
(Penguin), 1992

AUTHOR

David McKee

David McKee was born in 1916. Come *on*, he couldn't have worn *that* well! OK, it was 1944 in Calabria. Actually, it was 1935. No, that's a mistake. His parents were the only European couple in a band of Afghan brigands involved in something even now unknown; he was already five when he came to England in 1935, but that was recorded as his date of birth.

I'd heard something about Australia. Oh? Wasn't he a lonely, frail little boy, who got sent on long walks with a pencil and pad and told to draw? No, no – he used to be a ballet dancer, but lost the power in his legs, and started drawing when he was confined to bed.

Writers often say that they've told stories all their lives, but not everyone who's interviewed David recognises his actual lifestory's a story. "If everything is positive and known there's nothing left for your mind to play with – in my books I like to leave things unsaid, so that there's more than one way of taking it."

If it *really* matters, scattered clues suggest:– He's probably in his middle fifties. He's a Capricorn. He has a younger brother who as "an MG guru" can draw cars. He's long divorced but is close to his three grown-up children – the middle one, Chuck, told him the story of *The Mystery of the Blue Arrows* as they walked in the woods, and Brett, his younger son, has given him an SF story called "Moondogs" that he'd like to illustrate.

He lives in the south of France, because of the wonderful light ("In England I can see the paper, in France I can see the line"), on the seafront Promenade des Anglais in Nice because he loves watching all the people, and nipping over to Italy for lunch.

His accent says he is from south Devon – but then, so did his grandfather's, and *he* worked in a Scottish dockyard where he filled empty sherry barrels with his own illicit brew. A strong character, his grandad: he and David had children of the same age at the same time.

His army national service was sandwiched between Plymouth and Hornsey art colleges, and during it he managed to fit in a part-time course at Farnham. Aiming to be a painter but needing to earn a living, he was already selling cartoons while still at college, but, for a natural storyteller (as we know), a move into picture books seemed obvious. His first book, *Two Can Toucan,* was published in 1964; when it was reissued in 1985, new production techniques prompted him to reillustrate it – now the first is a collector's item he wishes he still had.

David says his picture books are for anyone, not only young children: from *King Rollo* to *Not Now, Bernard, Tusk Tusk* or *Elmer,* they tackle universal problems and relationships. Mr Benn was adopted by *Watch With Mother* long ago, and has now become immortal, his inner life as rich in stories as David's own; he's about to reappear in a technically challenging film that combines live actors with drawn backgrounds.

King Rollo gave his name to David's animated film company, now a successful role-model but an exciting risk to set up. The writer in him enjoys working with other artists like Tony Ross (their *Towser* cartoons have been going for years) or the Catalan artist, Carme Sole Vendrell, creator of Maria and the bear Victor. David once lived in Barcelona – he loves to travel, and can cheerfully tell stories in French, Italian and Spanish.

Which one you believe is up to you.

SELECTED TITLES

I Hate My Teddy Bear (Andersen), 1982

Two Monsters (Andersen), 1985

Snow Woman (Andersen), 1987

The Monster and the Teddy Bear (Andersen), 1989

Zebra's Hiccups (Andersen), 1991

Out of the Blue (Andersen), 1992

AUTHOR • ILLUSTRATOR

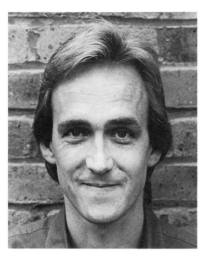

Photograph by Michael Ann Mullen

Colin McNaughton

Comics, *Beano* and *Dandy* annuals, Saturday morning cinema: these were the cultural influences of Colin McNaughton's childhood, ones which had a lasting effect on his own work. There were few books at home in Wallsend upon Tyne when he was growing up during the fifties and sixties.

His father was a pattern maker, a highly skilled craftsman in the shipyards. Colin, now among the most successful and admired children's artists in the country, was one of three children, and the black sheep of the family. He left home at sixteen ("walked out" said Colin; "thrown out" said his mother), but took care to stay near enough in Newcastle to go home with his dirty washing for Sunday lunch.

He *detested* school, so much so he couldn't talk about it for years. But he had one marvellous teacher, who introduced him to a Youth Theatre, something quite new for a boy from his background.

"Acting, costumes … absolutely marvellous if you've never known that kind of ability to express feelings before. It allowed me to break out of the scheme of things that had seemed set for boys like me – where you simply follow your father into the shipyards and so on."

It led to his choosing a foundation art course in Newcastle, followed by three years of graphic design at the Central School in London, and then three more years getting a Master's degree in illustration at the Royal College. His first books were published while still a student, and his degree show was made up entirely of published work.

He tried all sorts of editorial and advertising work,

but although the money was better than in children's publishing, the people and the "awful pecking order" were much less agreeable. He had married at nineteen, a pretty French girl who supported him through college and still handles his financial affairs. This meant he had to earn a decent living, so he was forced to produce books so quickly that he felt he could never offer his best work. Artists get a fairer deal today, and he is now as admired by the judges of top awards as he is loved by children. (But even slowing down, he has totalled over sixty titles in about fourteen years.)

Children have always recognised his talent, energy and humour – it was they rather than critics who turned *Football Crazy* into a classic. "Crazy" is a key word: it's an element that runs through all of his work, from his partnership with Allan Ahlberg in their *Happy Families* stories and *Red Nose Readers*, through to *Who's That Banging on the Ceiling?*. "The older I get the more I realise that my sense of humour is exactly the same as it was when I was four years old – it hasn't changed at all!"

But the craziness is that of a brilliantly inventive designer, one of the pioneers who have made the "comic strip" format as artistically respectable in Britain as in Europe, and it can conceal serious messages about, say, prejudice (*Have You Seen Who's Just Moved in Next Door to Us?*) or the environment (*Watch Out for the Giant Killers!*). For years he was tentative about writing, but blossomed out in such stories as *Jolly Roger* or verses like *There's An Awful Lot of Weirdos in Our Neighbourhood.*

Colin and Françoise have lived in almost as many London flats as he has produced books (perhaps not quite), but seem happily rooted now in Covent Garden, with two sons they say are "wild". Well, they would be, wouldn't they?

SELECTED TITLES

They Came From Aargh!, with Russell Hoban (Methuen), 1981

There's an Awful Lot of Weirdos in Our Neighbourhood (Walker), 1987

Fat Pig (A&C Black), 1987

Who's Been Sleeping in My Porridge? (Walker), 1990

The Pirats (Walker), 1992

Making Friends With Frankenstein (Walker), 1993

AUTHOR • ILLUSTRATOR

Michelle Magorian

Once upon a time, a young actress called Mikki Magorian was in Newcastle, appearing in *Joseph and the Amazing Technicolor Dreamcoat* and scribbling away in spare moments as usual. The lines "It was Red and Yellow and Green and Brown and..." sparked off some short stories suggested by the pairs of colours.

Two characters – a small boy, Willie Beech, a young "green" name, and a sturdy old countryman, "brown" Tom Oakley – seemed to have a life of their own, turning up in story after story. And if she could write stories, why not a novel? Eventually *Goodnight Mister Tom* took shape. She kept it secretly in a drawer until much later, when she shyly showed it to her tutor at some adult writing classes. *Goodnight Mister Tom,* by a young novelist who called herself Michelle Magorian, went on to win literary awards in Britain and America as well as top sales.

Michelle continued to write novels, short stories and two poetry collections for the young, and Mikki continued to act, on television, in pantomime farces and Young Vic tragedies. These days Michelle Magorian has developed a one-woman show which she takes round the country, using Mikki's skills to talk about Michelle's books and incorporate excerpts from them into a portrayal of life "in a leaky 1946 bedsitter". She has also written the book and lyrics of a musical adaptation of *Goodnight Mister Tom.* The two sides of Michelle Magorian's life have become truly entwined.

A tiny woman with a strong personality and the clear voice of an actor, she lives in the Wembley area of London with a husband who drives tanker lorries and their two sons, Tom and baby George. Her father was in the Navy, and she spent her childhood years in Singapore and Australia; it was elocution lessons designed to get rid of her Australian accent that opened up the world of drama to her.

At drama school she trained as a teacher as well as a performer (she hated teaching young people, but loves working with them), and studied mime with the legendary Marcel Marceau in Paris. It was during her years in repertory theatre that she lived the rosy Devon-or-Suffolk village life nostalgically described in all her novels.

Goodnight Mister Tom tells how a pathetic eight-year-old boy from London's East End at the start of the Second World War is evacuated to the countryside, to live with a crusty old widower, and how they come to love and depend on each other. The second novel, *Back Home,* about a girl evacuee returning to a bleak post-war England after five years in America, and third, *A Little Love Song,* about teenagers on the brink of adulthood during the war, are also set in the 1940s. Why, when Michelle herself was not even born then? She is still not sure, except that she became fascinated by the research on the details of daily life at that time; she thinks that after the fourth novel she really must re-enter the 1990s.

It was said that hardened printers cried as they worked on *Goodnight Mister Tom,* for there are scenes of brutality and grief as well as heart-warming happiness. What matters most to Michelle Magorian are people and their emotions, and from her characters' motives and relationships all else flows – plot, style, themes and ideas. Few contemporary writers have quite her ability to bring a lump to your throat, and make you sigh with wistful satisfaction as a book closes.

SELECTED TITLES

Goodnight Mister Tom
(Viking), 1981

Back Home
(Viking), 1985

Waiting For My Shorts to Dry (poetry)
(Viking), 1989

A Little Love Song
(Methuen), 1991

Orange Paw Marks
(poetry)
(Viking), 1991

Margaret Mahy

In March 1993, New Zealand awarded Margaret Mahy its highest honour, The Order of New Zealand, which only twenty living people can hold at any one time. This shows that a children's writer is regarded as highly in that country as, for instance, Sir Edmund Hillary, who conquered Mount Everest.

It's really a culmination of honours: among several international prizes, she has won the British Carnegie Medal twice, and the New Zealand equivalent, the Esther Glen Award, a record five times. Her publishers can hardly keep count of how many books – picture books, junior and teenage novels and collections of short stories – she's written, but it must be about seventy, and even that excludes dozens of titles for new readers. She is translated into at least fifteen languages.

But Margaret Mahy (you pronounce it Mah-hee) is an extraordinary woman. She has gone her own way all her life. She was born in 1936, the eldest of five children, with a huge extended family in the surrounding neighbourhood, and from the beginning her vivid imagination and love of storytelling sometimes confused reality and fantasy. She was a solitary little tomboy, living in her own world and talking out loud to herself. She knew she would be A Writer.

She sewed her made-up stories into little books, and would desperately try to make them come true. She would act out games that lasted a whole week and took over her life. Of course other children jeered at her when, for instance, she tried to convince them that she had magic powers and could speak to animals. But, although she was sometimes muddled and lonely, she had a cherished, happy childhood and

her parents never made her feel that eccentricity was something she should iron out of her life.

She studied philosophy at university in Auckland and Christchurch, and then qualified as a librarian, specialising in children's reading. She brought up her two daughters alone, which at that time meant life was often tough.

She had always written at night after work, and had some stories published in a journal issued to New Zealand schools. In 1968 Helen Hoke Watts, a famous American publisher, saw one (it became a classic picture book, *A Lion in the Meadow*) and asked for more; Margaret opened up her trunk and sent her a hundred – fifteen years of unpublished work. They were taken, she got a cheque for $1,000 (a fortune then – she bought a car), and she really was A Writer.

The need for money made her prolific but never stale. Her energy and fresh variety of styles are astonishing. The philosophical challenge she offers, particularly in her older teenage novels, even if it's sometimes puzzling, is always stimulating. As her daughters grew older, so did the material for her novels, but she has never abandoned her joyfully boisterous stories for younger readers, such as *The Great Piratical Rumbustification & The Librarian and the Robbers*.

Although she enjoys her own company, and lives alone in a house overlooking a harbour near Christchurch, she travels worldwide and talks with generous empathy to readers of all ages. And she is still fascinated by magic, mystery, witches and the supernatural, especially in her novels – *The Haunting* in 1982 was her first long work, followed by older ones like *The Changeover* and *The Tricksters*.

"It is in the nature of books," she says, "that they have the capacity to make you feel powerful about what you can alter and achieve in your life." She believed this when she was five; now she's proved it.

SELECTED TITLES

The Pirates' Mixed-Up Voyage
(Dent), 1983

The Downhill Crocodile Whizz and Other Stories
(Dent), 1986

Aliens in the Family
(Methuen), 1986

Underrunners
(Hamish Hamilton), 1992

The Dentist's Promise
(André Deutsch Children's Books), 1993

The Cousins quartet
(Doubleday), 1993

Photograph by Sabine Druce of Witney

Jan Mark

Art, not writing, had seemed Jan Mark's future. Her teacher steered her away from studying English at university because "you haven't got a scholar's brain" – which may explain why she failed an O level or two, but will surprise those who later came across her rather formidable intellect. But Jan agrees: she'd rather write her own books than research others. So instead she got a Diploma in Design from Canterbury College of Art.

Jan (short for Janet) had been born in Welwyn, Herts, moved into, then out of, London, and went to Ashford Grammar School in Kent. In the late sixties she taught in a Gravesend secondary school for six years – art at first, before switching after all to English. She married in 1969, moved to Norfolk and later had a son and daughter; they are now both grown up and the marriage itself is over. But they lived in Norfolk for fifteen years, and it is the setting of several of her stories, including *Thunder and Lightnings* (Lightnings were the great military jets that used to roar over the Norfolk countryside), *Under the Autumn Garden* and later *Handles*.

Thunder and Lightnings launched her. In 1975 the manuscript had won a *Guardian*/Penguin Books competition designed to discover new writers (they certainly found them – the runner-up was Anne Fine); when published it immediately won the country's top award, the Carnegie Medal. Within five years Jan and her husband had more or less swapped roles, and her writing became the family's financial support. And that is why, she says with a grim laugh, she writes only what is commissioned – adult novels are not commissioned, so she has only been able to afford to write one.

Jan Mark is lucky, however, that although the adult market for short stories is small, children enjoy them – "if only because they are short" – so she has been able to indulge her rare talent for the genre. It is one of the most demanding of writing techniques, and Jan tells teachers and struggling youngsters that it is daft to expect anyone, whether they are seven or forty-seven, to produce "a story" in a couple of hundred words as their first writing task.

In 1982 she worked for two years in schools with graduate student teachers, as writer-in-residence in the School of Education at Oxford Polytechnic. After five years of "uninterrupted writing in an empty room, in an empty house, eight hours a day", it was a joy to be involved with the life of students and colleagues, and the arguments and politics of an institution. A few years later she moved her home to Oxford as an ideal launchpad for all her travelling.

The name Jan Mark has come to be automatically associated with awards (including another Carnegie for *Handles*) over the whole age range, with her tough "heavies", the metaphysical SF trilogy of *Aquarius, Divide and Rule* and *The Ennead* straddling the borderline with adult novels at one end, and picture books like *Fur* and *Strat and Chatto* at the other. But in between are her most popular stories, compassionate, wittily truthful insights into life in and out of school.

She is admired not so much for her plots – which can be almost non-existent – as her brisk dialogue, character-revealing and very funny. She has written three plays, two for television and one from a story, *Captain Courage and the Rose Street Gang,* for school performance. She is a trenchant speaker herself, who enjoys school visits: the famously undisciplined hair overshadows mischievous but wary eyes which belie the sometimes dauntingly fierce expression. Like her work, she "can be deadly serious but funny too".

SELECTED TITLES

Nothing to be Afraid Of
(Viking), 1982

Hairs in the Palm of the Hand
(Viking), 1983

Feet and Other Stories
(Viking), 1983

Dream House
(Viking), 1987

The Twig Thing
(Viking), 1988

Man in Motion
(Viking), 1989

Ann M. Martin

The friends of Ann Martin love her devotedly. Shy but a good listener, a private person who has always disliked big social events, she chooses special friends carefully, but then never deserts them.

Beth Perkins is one of them. She and Ann grew up together on the same suburban road in the pleasant university town of Princeton, New Jersey. Its memories inspired "Stoneybrook, Connecticut" where the members of the Babysitters Club live; Kristy is a heightened version of Beth, and the Perkins girls are Beth's real-life daughters – except that they never get older.

Ann (her middle initial stands for her mother's maiden name, Matthews) was born in 1955. Her father is an artist and cartoonist who became well known in the *New Yorker* magazine, and the example of his self-discipline as a freelance has helped her cope with the fierce schedule that came with the gigantic success of *The Babysitters Club* – most writers would find it unbearably demanding to produce two best sellers a month!

But Ann has unexpected strength. She learnt how to deal with the nightmares she suffered as a little girl, with her own compelling drive to get top marks in as many subjects as possible right through school and university, with the "nervous stomach" that has always plagued her, and with the lifelong effects of an accident she had when she was eleven. She and a ladder crashed from a treehouse on to a stump, and the loss of her spleen damaged her immune system, and has led to recurring bouts of devastating tiredness and feeling very rotten. If possible, she tries to behave normally on her (quite frequent) bad days: "It helps me to think of myself as a relatively healthy person instead of a sick one. When I get up and concentrate on writing, I often feel better."

She studied education and psychology at the tough Smith College in Massachusetts, and for a year taught children with special needs. A temporary job in publishing led to six years as a children's editor. In 1980 she began her first book, *Bummer Summer*, eventually published three years later; she wrote four more while an editor, before risking full-time freelance editing and writing.

When a Scholastic editor suggested the idea of a babysitters' club, she had no way of knowing Ann was probably the best babysitter in the world! From a tiny girl she has adored children and had a genius for their entertainment and friendship (she is very close to the children of all her friends), and she started as a "mother's helper" at ten, developing into a sitter renowned for her patience and inventive care.

The first four Babysitters Club titles came in 1986 and 1987: today they appear in eighteen languages in at least twenty-one countries. They've led to the *Little Sister* series (because Ann was smitten with Karen, her "alter ego, who I wish I could be"), videos, a merchandising industry ranging from nightshirts to jigsaws, 15,000 fan letters a year, and a Foundation concerned with children, education, and the homeless. And Ann is involved in all of it.

So much in the books stems from her own life: the Kid-Kit notion, childhood summers in "Sea City", the death of her much-loved grandmother (*Claudia and the Sad Goodbye*), her younger sister Jane's dyslexia (*Claudia* perhaps, and *Yours Turly, Shirley*), while Mary Anne is, very loosely, herself. Now a celebrity, she is still anxious about people pressing in on her, but, as well as her New York flat off Fifth Avenue, she has an old country house – fourteen rooms and a tower – where she can be as silly as she likes with her old friends.

SELECTED TITLES

The Babysitters Club series
(Hippo), from 1988

Babysitters Specials series
(Hippo), from 1991

Babysitters Little Sister series
(Hippo), from 1991

The Babysitters Mysteries series
(Hippo), from 1993

Dear Babysitter. . . Letters From the Babysitters Club (Scholastic), 1994

AUTHOR

Michael Morpurgo

Photograph copyright © Katie Vandyck, 1993

If you stay at Nethercott Farm, you not only learn about country life – and wet work in the cowshed at 7.30 in the morning – but you meet Michael Morpurgo and maybe hear his latest tale.

Nethercott was the first of Michael and Clare Morpurgo's Farms for City Children twenty years ago. For thirty weeks in the year, this educational charity subsidises week-long visits by groups of about forty children, from schools who understand it's not just a mucking-about holiday. Each farm is different: Nethercott is in lush north Devon, *Tarka the Otter* country by the River Torridge (the Morpurgos live nearby), the second is "the last farm before America", high on windswept cliffs in Pembrokeshire, and the latest is an organic farm in gentle Gloucestershire.

Sweet-natured, boyish-faced and just turned fifty, Michael is a desirable grandfather – see *The Sandman and the Turtles* dedication. His family is soaked in the arts and education. One son's a painter, the other a writer, and daughter Ros works on the farm projects of which Clare is the business manager.

Clare and Michael met when he was eighteen "at a rubbish tip in Corfu". Michael's stepfather was director of the National Book League (forerunner of today's Book Trust), and Clare's father, Allen Lane, was the publishing genius who founded Penguins, the first paperbacks. The man who dreamed of bringing good books within the reach of everyone would today be happy that his legacy to his daughter is so vibrantly enriching the lives of city-bound youngsters.

Michael remembers only too well the enclosed world of the 1950s' school in *The War of Jenkins' Ear*.

He was born in London during the Second World War, and went to public schools in Sussex and Canterbury before Sandhurst Military Academy. "I'd been 'a good fellow' at school, played rugby, captained this and that, but left without an original thought in my head. I suddenly realised after six months that I was actually supposed to *kill* people! It was absurd, and I left to study English at London University instead. But it did knock the arrogant edges off me."

It was only after college, as a primary school teacher in the sixties, that he began to read for pure pleasure. Teaching, demonstrating around the farm, visiting schools – there's a performer behind his apparent shyness. "My real father was an actor in Canada, so it's in the blood." It was watching the excitement in children's eyes when he read to them that prompted Michael to think of writing himself. "But as a teacher I felt I wasn't having much impact on children's lives. I wanted to find a way of changing their perceptions of the world." This was the ideal behind the Farms project, but it's also the impulse for his books.

He has written over forty, for early teens or younger, been translated into a dozen languages, and has steadily climbed to the top of the popularity ratings. *Why the Whales Came* and *My Friend Walter* have been filmed, and he appears (tantalisingly) on every prize shortlist.

Entertaining stories, yes, and always touching, but each carries its readers to a different time and place, confronts them with some of the tough moral choices life will have in store for them, and tries to foster peace and tolerance. Even Michael's younger animal stories take a quietly moral line.

"There's an elemental thing that makes young children and animals understand each other. Animals bring out a sense of fairness, of what's right, in children – I see this all the time."

SELECTED TITLES

War Horse
(Kaye & Ward), 1982

Twist of Gold
(Heinemann), 1983

King of the Cloud Forests
(Heinemann), 1987

Mr Nobody's Eyes
(Heinemann) 1989

Waiting for Anya
(Methuen), 1991

The Marble Crusher
(Heinemann), 1992

Jill Murphy

When you're only eighteen and three major publishers tell you that your book is boring, you do tend to get discouraged, and think that perhaps you were wrong about its being so wonderful. So Jill Murphy put *The Worst Witch* away in a drawer. It was eventually published in 1974 – and more than a million customers have proved Jill wasn't wrong.

Jill Murphy was born and grew up with an older brother in Chessington, Surrey, but went to the Ursuline convent school in Wimbledon. Her father also had a talent for drawing but worked in an aircraft factory where it was never given a chance. Her mother, who had been a librarian at Harrods (which used to run a famous lending library), had dreamed of being a writer herself and found it irresistible to encourage her bright little daughter. And Jill turned out to have an "absolute drive" that made her an ace storyteller by the time she went to school.

But later, at her strict and formally academic convent, she wrote only secretly at home. The school didn't really know what to do with her – she thinks she was "unpigeonholeable" – and were only too pleased when at sixteen she opted for a foundation course at Chelsea Art School. After a second foundation year at Croydon Art School she went on to Camberwell, where she lasted for just one term before she and all art schools parted company. The illustration courses she wanted hadn't been invented at that time – and anyway, she thought of herself as primarily a writer.

For a while she worked as a nanny and in a children's home, which she loved and would even now happily return to: she deeply appreciates children, and relishes school visits. Less jolly were such ill-paid freelance tasks as providing 512 outline drawings for a colouring book. She has been married twice, lived ten years in Cornwall, seasonally in and out of "winter-lets" before affording her own cottage, and now lives in an almost-rural Garden Suburb in north London with four-year-old Charlie.

She was twenty-four when she met Clive Allison and Margaret Busby at a party. They were the young partners of a new publishing company who didn't even do children's books, but perhaps they were drawn to her long-haired hippy looks at that time and the puppy under her arm? She hopefully fished out *The Worst Witch,* they published it, and it got rave reviews.

In hardback and paperback, it's been reprinted thirty-eight times in twenty years; unusually, it has sold almost entirely in Britain – most best-sellers need international boosting. Fan letters begged for more about the escapades of Mildred, struggling to get her witching grades, and Jill followed with *The Worst Witch Strikes Again.* The comic clash of fantasy and reality in a classic school-story setting seems to grip youngsters with reading problems as strongly as avid bookworms.

It was the necessity to work only in line, with no colour shading, that meant Miss Cackle's Academy had to be entirely black and white. So Jill welcomed the chance to work with coloured pencils, with which she's more comfortable, on her first picture book, *Peace At Last,* an immortal account of parental desperation that bred another line of best sellers. And it's her picture books that have brought her awards – as well as American sales.

She says her ideas never come from "outside" her: Mildred's school-days echo her own, and her elephant family is based on that of a friend who's just had her fifth baby – and her last, Jill hopes, because she's running out of space on the page.

SELECTED TITLES

Worst Witch books
(Allison & Busby; Viking),
from 1974

Five Minutes' Peace
(Walker), 1986

Worlds Apart
(Walker), 1988

A Piece of Cake
(Walker), 1989

Geoffrey Strangeways
(Walker), 1990

A Quiet Night In
(Walker), 1993

AUTHOR • ILLUSTRATOR

Grace Nichols

"One of the best memories I have of myself is standing up to my calves in the sunlit water, watching the shapes of fish go by and every now and then cupping my own hands underneath and feeling the slippery fish slip through my fingers."

Grace Nichols was born in Guyana, the little Caribbean country on the edge of South America, in a rural village by the sea called Highdam – a name that suggests the brown water that came swirling in after heavy rain before being drained away.

She was one of a family of seven children (just one boy!); their father was a headteacher and she remembers how well their mother played the piano. When Grace was eight they moved to the capital, Georgetown. At sixteen she was already a student teacher, starting a three-year training; she went on to college in Baltimore, in America, but came home after six months when her mother died. She became a journalist on a national paper, the *Chronicle,* married and had a daughter who is now grown-up.

She enjoyed this period, choosing her own themes for feature articles – subjects whose general concerns are still with her, such as the market women telling her about their lives. She went on to work for the government information services, and took a university course in Communications.

On a personal level, it was fiction that interested her then: her first poem sprang from the sight of a waterfall on a survey fieldwork trip into the interior of the country. Most Guyanese live along the coast, and never see the vast rivers which come down from their rugged border mountains to cut through a forest canopy that stretches to the horizon. That was the most exciting journey of her life, and even after twelve years, far away in England, the memory could still spark the poem "For Forest".

She had come here in 1977 with her countryman and fellow-poet, John Agard. They brought with them the rhythms, the words and music, of their distant tropical childhoods, to warm the lives of the children of chilly England. For a few months they lived with John's dad in London, making ends meet with freelance writing until they became established names, but now they live in Sussex. Although they often perform together, and are an essential element of any Caribbean cultural celebration (there must surely be times when the Agard-Nichols household is really jumpin'), each has a strong individual identity.

Grace has continued to write prose – a novel for adults and short stories (*Leslyn in London*) for children – but is best known as a poet. In 1983 she won the prestigious Commonwealth Poetry Prize for the adult *I Is a Long-Memoried Woman* (she remains intensely concerned with the role of women, their feelings and problems).

She is also highly regarded as an anthologist. *Black Poetry* and *Can I Buy a Slice of Sky?* were stimulating injections into our cultural bloodstream, alerting young English-speakers, black and white, to the richness of their worldwide heritage.

If your parents are poets, you may be lucky enough to have your name made up specially for you! And although when *Come On Into My Tropical Garden* was published in 1988, Kalera was not yet born, it must now seem to her that her mother had written those poems, too, especially for her, making her a brightly wrapped present of her childhood. What is wonderful is that all other children also feel that – it will surely remain the best-loved of Grace Nichols' work.

SELECTED TITLES

Trust You Wriggly
(Hodder & Stoughton),
1980

Leslyn in London
(Hodder & Stoughton),
1984

Black Poetry (ed)
(Blackie), 1988

*Come on Into My
Tropical Garden**
(A&C Black), 1988

Can I Buy a Slice of Sky?
(ed) (Blackie), 1991

*No Hickory, No Dickory,
No Dock,*
with John Agard
(Viking), 1991

*Published by Puffin as
Poetry Jump-Up*

Helen Oxenbury

When John Burningham, whom we meet elsewhere in this book, was at the Central School of Art in London he met a younger fellow student, Helen Oxenbury. They hadn't known it, but they had gone to school a few miles from each other.

Helen had hated hers in Ipswich, prim, all girls and very Victorian, and survived only through the holidays and weekends spent roaming the coast at home in Felixstowe. "I love that scenery – the clear light, the strip of land, the huge sky, the wheeling birds and the mudflats." She and John still have a boathouse on the estuary.

She did, however, relish the hard work of Ipswich Art School, and in the vacations provided the slave labour for painting sets at the Repertory Theatre, which she enjoyed so much she decided on theatre design as a career. She went on to the Central School, where, if she'd understood, she might have foreseen her future. A tutor in costume design told her she should turn to illustration, because it was faces that really involved her: "You're more interested in the character and we don't *know* who's going to play the part!"

Following John, she went to Israel, designing huge backdrops for a famous Tel Aviv theatre. Three years later she came home to work in television and film studios, before marrying John. She was watching him with *Borka,* expecting her first child and needing money, when a friend, Jan Pieńkowski, suggested she design cards for his Gallery Five, and then try a baby book – something she could manage at home. *Numbers of Things* was immediately accepted, and she has never stopped since.

Five years after John, she too won the Kate

Greenaway Medal for illustrating Edward Lear and Margaret Mahy, and has gone on winning prizes for books like *We're Going on a Bear Hunt* and *Farmer Duck*. She has around sixty titles to her name – many are baby books that come in series – and is an international bestseller.

It used to be the fashion to believe that small children's eyes and brains saw in a different, limited, way, and that their pictures therefore had to be symbolically simple, like Dick Bruna's *Miffy* books. The huge success of Helen Oxenbury's board books showed that even young babies could appreciate action, movement and humour. She had begun a style revolution.

When she began illustrating books the family lived in a tiny flat, so she used crayons, pen and ink because they took up little space. She did *Pig Tale* in gouache (like poster paint), then moved on to watercolour (difficult because if you go wrong you have to scrap it and start again), and is always ready to experiment and change. She loves black and white line, and grieves that the sales force of publishers always want colour.

Her son and daughter were teenagers when her second daughter was born, and the new baby's growing up was mirrored in the sort of books her mother was drawing – Helen was sad when she finally left illustrated books behind. She enjoys working on the stories of other writers, but not working *with* them – she had never even met Michael Rosen until the party when *Bear Hunt* won the Smarties Prize.

She recognises at once a story she'll be comfortable with, rejecting hundreds on the way. The recipe is the same as for her own books: "It must have warmth and humour and be true to life, and, above all, characters that are not absolutely wonderful and lovely!"

SELECTED TITLES

The Quangle Wangle's Hat, by Edward Lear (Heinemann), 1969

Pig Tale (Heinemann), 1973

Heads, Bodies and Legs trio (Walker), 1980

First Picture Books series (Walker), 1984

Pippo series (Walker), 1988-9

We're Going on a Bear Hunt, with Michael Rosen (Walker), 1989

AUTHOR • ILLUSTRATOR

Philippa Pearce

One hot summer, Philippa Pearce was recovering from tuberculosis but was not yet well enough to leave hospital in Cambridge. She brightened the long days in bed by savouring in her imagination every second of a canoe trip on the river that had run beside the garden of her childood home, thirty years before. Later, convalescing, she wove those memories into *Minnow on the Say* which, after being rejected by one (soon to be sorry) publisher, became a runner-up for the Carnegie Medal.

Philippa was the youngest of two boys and two girls whose father was a flour-miller in Great Shelford, a village on the upper, smaller, reaches of the River Cam, just five miles from that hospital bed. *His* father had been the miller before him, and he had grown up in the Mill House, moving back with his young family when he took over the mill.

This countryside appears in many of Philippa's stories, the village becoming Great Barley and the river, the Say. In *Tom's Midnight Garden* (the Carnegie winner of 1959 and one of the greatest children's novels ever written), Tom plays in the same garden as his little nineteenth-century friend, just as Philippa had played in the same garden as her father. Indeed, both *are* the same garden, the very one we see in the book's chapter-heads.

Philippa's was the first generation in her family to go into higher education – three of the children won scholarships to university. She studied English and history at Cambridge, and was briefly a civil servant until the war finished. Then she worked for thirteen years as a scriptwriter and producer in the Schools Broadcasting Department of the BBC, and it was during a year's leave because of her illness that she began writing her own fiction.

Looking back, she recognised that to write words for people to speak is the most splendid training, and now she always advises new writers to "read aloud in your head". Being confined to 3,000 words in twenty-minute bursts honed her talent for short stories, and she became renowned for her disciplined, pared-down style, but it also meant she revelled in the luxury of novels.

She hoped an editorial post with the academic side of the Oxford University Press would compensate for her lack of teaching experience with children, but she quickly realised it was a wrong move, and returned to London in 1960 to become the children's editor at publishers André Deutsch. She combined this with freelance writing and producing a weekly radio programme, *The World of Books* – a work-load that produced teeth-clenching tension.

In 1963 Philippa married Martin Christie, a fruit grower. Martin died suddenly the following year, largely as a result of his years in a Japanese prisoner-of-war camp, but he had had the joy of welcoming his daughter Sally, although she was only eight weeks old when her father died.

Animals – a goat and pony, cats, dogs, hens and gerbils – have been as much a part of their lives as of the books (the gerbils in *The Battle of Bubble and Squeak* won the Whitbread Award!). Indeed, instead of cutting down when Sally left home, Philippa finds herself thinking of even the hens as somewhat eccentric companions she would be sad to lose. She is back in "Great Barley", in a cottage her grandfather built, the Mill House and riverside garden close by but changed with the years. Does that hurt? Not at all, she says, with the gentle wisdom of her books – the years have changed her too.

SELECTED TITLES

A Dog So Small
(Constable), 1962

The Elm Street Lot
(Viking), 1969

What the Neighbours Did and Other Stories
(Longman), 1972

Shadow-Cage
(Kestrel), 1977

The Way to Sattin Shore
(Kestrel), 1983

Old Belle's Summer Holiday
(André Deutsch Children's Books), 1989

AUTHOR

K.M. Peyton

Photograph copyright © Evening Echo, Basildon, Essex

It's a miracle that Kathleen Peyton found time to write one book, far less over forty. She constantly promises herself a break, but the compulsion (and she says it *is* a compulsion) always returns – she doesn't know why.

Neither does she know where her passion for horses came from. Long before she was ten, her bike had become a noble chestnut hunter called Talisman, or, if she had to walk, she "rode" one of the *two thousand* imaginary horses she had listed in exercise books, and whose stories she wrote up in the evenings.

Yet this was a girl whose family were engineers and shopkeepers, living in the suburbs south of London, and travelling by train throughout the war (once they were machine-gunned from a plane) to Wimbledon High School. Her dream was to be an artist, not a writer, but all the time she was secretly sending novels to the publisher of her favourite pony books – the kindly rejection notes only encouraged her. When she was fifteen she illustrated one for an art project, and her teacher had the apparently startling idea of finding a publisher. *Sabre, the Horse from the Sea* was published a year later, with the next already accepted.

The war ended (Kathleen truanted on Talisman to go to the first peacetime race at Epsom), and the family's move north meant she transferred to Manchester School of Art. Homesick without her friends, she was happy only when walking on the windswept hills. The college itself was over-crowded with returned soldiers trying to pick up their lives. One, an ex-prisoner of war who had escaped and fought for the Russians, who "wasn't a wow to look at" because lack of food had made clumps of his hair fall out, loved roaming the hills too. Michael Peyton was twenty-six, Kathleen seventeen. As soon as she was twenty-one they married, and for four months roamed the untamed places of Europe together.

It was the start of a life crazily overflowing with material for a writer. Kathleen got a degree and taught art for two years and Mike was an illustrator and cartoonist, but they also canoed, climbed mountains and lived wild without a tent throughout Europe and Canada, sometimes cold and hungry and occasionally in danger.

In 1956 they finally settled in an isolated spot by the tidal estuary of the Crouch in Essex. They took up sailing – with their two small daughters they once abandoned ship in a North Sea storm – and Mike made his name as *the* yachting cartoonist. And at last, in her thirties, Kathleen had her first real-life pony; she has never been without horses since, becoming deeply involved in the Pony Club and even buying a quarter of a racehorse. When most people retire, the Peytons were riding coast-to-coast through Scotland.

Throughout this time Kathleen was producing a whole range of books – histories, romances, comedies, psychological suspense, but all terrific stories. Tales of the estuary's past, such as *The Maplin Bird* or the First World War *Thunder in the Sky*, led to the award-winning series, *Flambards,* and television fame; a sixth-form yob she saw on a train, who proved to be a local hero, suggested the *Pennington* books (her favourites); racing gave material for novels like *Dear Fred.*

This small, slight, self-deprecating woman will never stop, in spite of mucking out horses every morning, and dealing with fifteen acres of land, woods and garden. But she still insists that art is what she loves best – she relishes her little Cartwheel books because she also illustrates them. Writing, she says, is simply more convenient.

SELECTED TITLES

A Midsummer Night's Death
(Oxford), 1978

Who, Sir? Me, Sir?
(Oxford), 1983

Downhill All the Way
(Oxford), 1988

The Boy Who Wasn't There
(Doubleday), 1992

The Wild Boy and Queen Moon
(Doubleday), 1993

Snowfall
(André Deutsch Children's Books), 1994

Terry Pratchett

"Too much navel-gazing is bad for you," says Terry Pratchett.

But he thinks there may be something in the theory that links his childhood, "a more or less idyllic Richmal Crompton one [she wrote *Just William*] in what was then a very rural village", with the fantasy worlds he has created. These "tend to be enclosed ones which are either threatened (usually the Discworld) or are a base from which the greater universe is explored (*Truckers*)."

This childhood was around Beaconsfield, Bucks, where Terry was born in 1948. He was transformed into an avid reader by discovering *The Wind in the Willows* when he was ten, and by the time he was thirteen he'd sold his first story to *Science Fantasy* magazine and spent the £14 fee on a typewriter. So it seemed natural to leave school at seventeen and work in local journalism while continuing to write. He was a committed SF fan, meeting professional writers at conventions where fans are encouraged "to get your hands dirty and write, and are not made to feel writers are a different breed."

He was twenty when he published his first novel, *The Carpet People*. It sold reasonably, but nothing special: in 1992, "co-written" by Pratchett aged seventeen and Pratchett aged forty-three, with a few extra bits ("My imagination has always been pretty much the same, but I've learned to steer it better"), it was a children's best seller. Now the original book, in good condition, could fetch £250. Terry Pratchett has become a household name.

But that took time. In his thirties he began to worry about his future, and jumped over the journalistic fence to become a press officer for the Central

AUTHOR

Electricity Generating Board. The paperback success of his fourth novel, the first of the *Discworld* stories, suggested it was safe to give up his job. In 1987 he became a full-time writer.

These days Terry produces two or three books a year. His ability to be richly funny and exciting at the same time, to anchor his soaring imagination and eccentric characters in agreeable sentiment and prophet-like wisdom, propels all his novels into the best-seller lists. His children's books are among the very few – joining Roald Dahl's, *Adrian Mole* and *Fighting Fantasies* – to appear among the adult top sellers of any given year, while young readers can be as enthralled by his *Discworld* series as adults.

Terry and his wife Lyn, who used to be a teacher, live with their teenage daughter Rianna in a 300-year-old cottage near Cheddar Gorge and the Mendip Hills. Writing has pretty well taken over his life, but he hangs on to some of his hobbies, such as growing carnivorous plants and the Japanese miniature trees called bonsai, and fooling around giving sophisticated add-ons to out-dated computers. Some people find him a bit alarming – he says in real life he's training to be Victor Meldrew (the exasperating old boy in *One Foot in the Grave*) – but his signing sessions around the country are prodigious, and he has become a familiar figure in his splendid hats: "I can't walk past a good hat shop."

The Johnny Maxwell books reach out to fantasy from the real world. "I like Johnny. I like the way he's constantly trying to get to grips with the universe." Whether as a rainforest frog in a puddle on a leaf, or as a bouncing pinball, getting to grips with the proportions of a universe which always has one more universe outside it is a recurring Pratchett theme. There will be more books about Johnny Maxwell, he promises. And, no doubt, more about the universe.

SELECTED TITLES

The *Truckers* Trilogy
(Doubleday), 1989

The Carpet People
(Doubleday), 1992

Only You Can Save Mankind
(Doubleday), 1992

Johnny and the Dead
(Doubleday), 1993

Frank Rodgers

With twenty-three books in five years – there'll be more by the time you're reading this – Frank Rodgers is a man in a hurry. This lanky Scot thinks he's inherited his mad energy from his mother (she's the granny in *The Bunk-Bed Bus*).

We're counting his own books; adding those he has only illustrated brings it to fifty. Partly because he was a late starter and feels that he must catch up, and partly because it's such a joyful life compared with struggling in a job where he was uncomfortable, Frank is one of the most workaholic but chipper authors around.

He was born and grew up in Holytown, a village in what was then genuine country outside Glasgow where he lives today. His father was, among other things, a clock-repairer; a talented man who suffered from ill health, he might have become an artist himself. Frank had two younger sisters, but only he was famous for his doodles and daft scripts – even at twelve he was up on stage entertaining with his funny drawings.

Like every other teenager in the late fifties, he was a *Goon Show* and *Journey Into Space* addict, a product of radio and a library system that had given him everything from comics to classics. This was the period he relives in *The Drowning Boy* (1992), his first teenage, unillustrated, novel. That eerie ruined house did exist, and in real life seventeen-year-old Frank was also bound for Glasgow School of Art. There he met Liz, the girl he would marry.

He can't now explain why he specialised in silversmithing and jewellery, oddly old-fashioned subjects for his comic talent, but after he'd left college he remembered the stuff he used to do at school and sent off an illustrated rhyming story to a publisher. "It was rejected, of course, and I took the huff – for twelve years."

Instead he taught art, cheering up life with music. He composed and performed on guitar and piano, writing rock musicals for his school and songs for a band. A contract with Island Records seemed to promise something more than school-teaching, and he, the band and Liz (who was expecting Zoë) set off for London.

But no. After two years of gigs in pubs and being a hired-car driver (colliding with the back of a truck while squinting at the A-Z map), he came home to Glasgow and teaching again. Yet a seed had been sown. He'd had such fun illustrating a book by a flamboyant character he'd met in London – publishers loved the pictures but not the book – that he put together an "instant" portfolio and set off again next year. And it worked!

He designed his first book jacket around 1977, and in the early years illustrated other writers, famously Humphrey Carpenter and the *Mr Majeika* stories. He was still involved in music – one of his rock musicals, *Think of the Magic*, was published and is still performed widely. "I love visualising things on stage." Then in 1987 he daringly demanded a collective advance fee for three of his picture book ideas, *Who's Afraid of the Ghost Train?*, *A is for AAARGH!* and *The Bunk-Bed Bus*, which gave him the financial launch-pad out of teaching.

His *My First Monster* books arrive, like buses, in fours; they've brought exciting merchandising deals for greetings cards and toys on a worldwide scale. The future's bright: Zoë's at university; son Adam is fifteen and looks set to be an artist too; Liz, who once owned a contemporary art gallery, is a painter herself. Frank can't imagine running out of ideas – and Granny's set the pace.

SELECTED TITLES

The Bunk-Bed Bus
(Viking), 1989

A is for Aaargh!
(Viking), 1989

B is for Book
(Viking), 1992

The Drowning Boy
(André Deutsch
Children's Books), 1992

Comic Fun
(Hippo), 1992

My First Monster books
(Hippo), 1993-4

Michael Rosen

Photograph by Graham Dunn

Long face and beard; round, round eyes and eyebrows raised high enough to crash into the shaggy hair; tall gangling body, arms flung wide with star-hands at the end, like a four-year-old's drawing – it's not often a poet is instantly recognised by every kid in the land. But Michael Rosen is as exuberant a performer as he is a poet, on television, in a concert hall or classroom – even invisibly on radio.

In fact, at Oxford University, he was as involved with the theatre – writing, directing and acting in plays – as with his English studies, and certainly more than with poetry. He'd been a medical student at the Middlesex Hospital in London for a year before he realised his mistake and re-routed himself to Oxford.

Born in 1946, he grew up in the London suburb of Harrow with a brother who is now a marine ecologist; their parents, both teachers, were well-known and respected figures in the world of books, politics and education. "Somehow or another my parents were able to manage a combination of being terribly bothered about me and at the same time give me an enormous amount of space." He remembers them and his childhood with great affection and respect – but not the school system of that time, which seemed to have the passing of tests and exams as its single, deadening, goal.

Somewhere between reading James Joyce's *A Portrait of the Artist as a Young Man* and watching his mother put together poetry magazine programmes for educational radio, Mike discovered a new writing voice – the voice of the child he once was. He was encouraged by his mother's BBC producer to such an extent that he eventually took over his mum's job for a few years – he doesn't know how she felt about this.

It was a voice young readers instantly tuned into. *Mind Your Own Business* was published in 1974 and is still a best seller. Since then books – his own poems, anthologies he has edited, and stories – have poured out of him, while he continues to broadcast and visit schools.

He is passionately committed to helping children to find their *own* voices, to realise that they do have something to say, and that how they themselves would say it is as rich and worthwhile as any adult's "proper" way. Adult reaction to this and to his work swings between accusing him of not writing Poetry (capital P) and awarding him some of Britain's top prizes.

He and his wife Geraldine live in Hackney, in east London, with the living proof of how he feels about kids – five children, two of whom are from his previous marriage. Like many writers, the age-range of his books has kept pace with his children, through the middle years in *When Did You Last Wash Your Feet?* to *Culture Shock*. Language belongs to everyone, he is saying, to be played with and enjoyed as well as respected. His prose is as vigorous as his verse, sometimes fooling around with words and familiar tales, turning them into *Hairy Tales and Nursery Crimes* or *Arabian Frights and other Gories* (with Annie Ha-Ha and the Forty Steves), sometimes paying homage to tradition (*The Wicked Tricks of Till Owlyglass*), sometimes blending creepy horror with farce, in the short stories of *Nasty!*

What he loves best is making people laugh. But beyond all the bounce and jokes there is a tenacious public campaigner for education, and for freedom and equality in society as a whole. Michael Rosen *looks* like a wild radical, and he'd be proud to be called one.

SELECTED TITLES

Wouldn't You Like to Know
(André Deutsch Children's Books), 1977

You Can't Catch Me
(André Deutsch Children's Books), 1981

We're Going on a Bear Hunt, with Helen Oxenbury
(Walker), 1989

The Golem of Old Prague, with Val Biro
(André Deutsch Children's Books), 1990

Mind the Gap
(Scholastic), 1992

Action Replay
(Viking), 1993

Tony Ross

Tony Ross reckons he's a lucky man, earning a good living at what he enjoys most. "Yes, I do a lot of work, but it isn't really *work*. Carrying bricks – that's work; going down pits, digging farmland on cold mornings – that's work. But sitting in a studio doing little drawings – that's marvellous!"

In fact, he's unbelievably industrious, and his own books, animated films and illustrations for other writers seem to be everywhere you look. As well as being popular in Britain, his work wins awards all over Europe and is translated into at least fifteen languages. (Towser the dog is called Mackintosh in France, Rudolpho in Spain…) Picture books like *The Boy Who Cried Wolf* or *I Want My Potty* are now universal classics, while popular stories by other writers, like Philip Curtis's *Mr Browser* series or Hazel Townson's new readers, are unimaginable without his drawings.

He works so quickly that he often finishes a book before the publisher has worked out the contract: he says he is himself honest and so he trusts other people, and, in any case, doesn't put a crude money-value on his work. If something goes wrong, "I'll do another drawing – I'm not dead yet." So it's not surprising that he enjoys presenting modern, very personal, versions of fairy tales, with their timeless and symbolic morals.

When he was young it was horses, not art, that filled his dreams. At seventeen he wrote to John Wayne, offering to make his own way over if he could just be in a western. There was no reply. He reckons it's still the Wayne-syndrome, the dazzle of the stage (father a conjuror, uncles as film extras), that makes him love to put on an act in his talking-and-drawing sessions with groups of kids.

Although he was born in Wandsworth, south London, he moved to Cheshire as a small boy during the war. So, despairing of horses, it was to Liverpool Regional College of Art he went, because, he says, he wasn't up to anything else. (That is about as true as his claim that he always draws big eyes because he can't draw real eyes!)

He had a go at all sorts of work when he left – even chemical factories and building sites – before becoming art director in an advertising agency. After one specially bad day there, he turned to teaching, becoming senior lecturer at Manchester Polytechnic – several of our best artists owe a lot to him as friend and tutor.

He lives in a late-Georgian house, just on the edge of Macclesfield, with Zoë, his third wife and business partner, who watches over his affairs so efficiently he can maintain his faith in the niceness of other people, and with Kate, the last of three daughters and a son to be still at home.

His illustrations for one of the Moonlight Discoverers guides, *Painting*, are a reminder that his art is far more varied than the spiky cartoon style associated with his name. There, he had the fun of copying works of the great masters: "Some were very easy – the old chaps I admire like Michelangelo and Leonardo, and the Magrittes just rolled off – but others were impossible, like Turner and Rembrandt."

His own style has affinities with Edward Lear (subject of his student thesis) and the caricaturist Rowlandson, and he rejoices in the freedom he has, as artist, designer, and typographer, to control his own page. "I like the form of a book to *do* things, the covers and endpapers to add point, make the reader puzzle and be excited."

SELECTED TITLES

Towser series
(Andersen), 1985

The Boy Who Cried Wolf
(Andersen), 1985

The Happy Rag
(Andersen), 1990

A Fairy Tale
(Andersen), 1991

Don't Do That
(Andersen), 1991

I Want to Be
(Andersen), 1993

AUTHOR • ILLUSTRATOR

Maurice Sendak

It was Christmas, Maurice Sendak was twenty-one or so, and working as a window-designer in a famous New York toyshop, F.A.O. Schwarz; he decided to "draw his face off", and filled the whole shop-front with drawings from *A Christmas Carol*. It was "like putting a huge hook in the water and waiting for a fish to be caught". A publishing editor rose to the bait, commissioned his first work, and became a lifelong friend.

At that time, Maurice (pronounced the French way – Maureece) was getting the only formal art training he's ever had by attending night school for two years. While in high school (which he hated), he had worked for All-American Comics, but in 1948, when he was twenty, he and his elder brother began to make animated wooden toys, which led to the Schwarz job.

He had been a very sickly child ("I learned early on that it was a very chancy business, being alive") and missed a lot of school. He was the youngest of three, so his sister Natalie, nine years older, was always having to look after him, and he remembers both how much she loved him and how angry she used to get. *Outside Over There*, the last of the trilogy that began with *Where the Wild Things Are* and *In the Night Kitchen*, is his most personal book, and his favourite; it is really a tribute to Natalie, "who is Ida, very brave, very strong, very frightening, taking care of me. Baby."

Maurice, son of a hard-up dressmaker, grew up in Brooklyn, across the river from New York City. Everyone in his family told stories, remembered gruesome fairy tales and Jewish folklore, and drew pictures. His father, the son of a rabbi, had run away from home and been disowned when he went to America, but his mother's family was so poor that at sixteen they had *sent* her to America, and she had worked in sweatshops so that she could bring over her mother and brothers.

Maurice's other childhood influence was the cinema – three Oliver Hardys and King Kong turn up in *In the Night Kitchen*. And the boy Mickey. Mickey Mouse was born six months after Maurice Sendak, and he has been obsessed with him ever since: his pretty 1790 New England house, set amid the woodland of Connecticut, is crammed with Mickey Mouse collectors' items.

Here he lives alone, looking after his dog (Jennie from *Higglety Pigglety Pop!* was a much-loved Sealyham), and working seven days a week with a scrupulously tidy, ordered routine. Since 1951 he has published over eighty titles, mainly with other authors – such as the *Little Bear* stories, *Mr Rabbit and the Lovely Present*, or *I Saw Esau* – and is recognised worldwide as one of the greatest illustrators of all time. But it is his own books, though far fewer, which have brought him international awards and academic honours. Since the 1970s he has also become an acclaimed opera designer and, for operas derived from his own books, librettist.

In the Night Kitchen has a secret. Visiting England in 1967, Maurice had a severe heart attack live on camera in the middle of a Tyne Tees chat show. He woke up in the Queen Elizabeth Hospital, Gateshead, totally puzzled to hear a nurse encouraging him with "Champion! Champion!" Three years later the nursing staff each received a thank-you copy of *In the Night Kitchen*: in the Manhattan skyline one of the cartons is inscribed "Q.E. Gateshead" and one of the bottles has "CHAMPION" on its little flag.

SELECTED TITLES

Chicken Soup With Rice
(in Nutshell Library)
(Collins), 1964

Little Bear Books,
by Else Minarik
(World's Work), 1965

Where the Wild Things Are
(The Bodley Head), 1967

Hector Protector
(The Bodley Head), 1967

The Sign on Rosie's Door
(The Bodley Head), 1970

Seven Little Monsters
(The Bodley Head), 1977

AUTHOR • ILLUSTRATOR

117

Robert Swindells

More than anything, Bob Swindells wishes his mum could see him now.

She died in 1966 of multiple sclerosis, a distressingly slow death that traumatised Bob. Before too many children and too little money were to sap her time and energy, she had taught him as a toddler to read. In years to come he escaped from everyday miseries and his parents' quarrels into a world of fantasy and books. But never, ever, did he or his mother dream *he* could become both a teacher and an author!

Born in Bradford, he was six months old when the war started in 1939. His father, a travelling salesman who in any case was often away from home, was drafted into the RAF. Bob spent the war years in the country just outside Bradford with his mother and baby brother; by the time he was ten he had two more brothers and a sister.

He failed the "eleven-plus" exam that would have given him entry to grammar school, and in those days this ended his dreams of being a teacher. But his disappointment and powerless rage at his father's humiliating taunts were to have an unexpected effect on his life. And his tough secondary modern school did have one special teacher who sowed the idea that he could write – Bob "recognised" him instantly in the film *Dead Poets Society*.

He left school at fifteen and was for two years a copyholder on the local newspaper, reading out the original material to the proof-readers. This proved a real education, for the proof-readers were knowledgeable men who enjoyed playing around with language. But Bob was finding life impossible with his father (and seven people in a three-bedroomed

AUTHOR

house), and signed up for three years in the RAF, serving as a clerk in Germany.

Back home he rejoined the paper and married a local girl; by the time he was twenty-three and Cathy eighteen they had two daughters, Linda and Jill. It was when the man who collected their weekly insurance money said he was leaving to train as a teacher, that Bob realised he too might still fulfil his boyhood dream. He changed to an undemanding factory job, took O levels at night school, and at twenty-nine was accepted by a college in Huddersfield.

Life was transformed. He discovered great writers and children's novels, and revelled in them all. He was *not* a failure! Then, for his graduating thesis, he daringly wrote his own children's novel, set in the Stone Age; not only did he pass, but the examiner recommended some publishers' names. As in a fairy tale, *When Darkness Comes* (1973) was immediately accepted – and even reissued twenty years on.

Six years and five books later Bob cut down his teaching, and in 1980 left it altogether to become a full-time writer. By then he had grown a long way from the boy who had married Cathy; they finally parted and each remarried. Today Bob lives with Brenda in the Brontë country of the Pennines, and has three grandchildren.

In 1984 the post-nuclear *Brother in the Land* had an explosive impact on critics, prize panels and young readers alike: with it and *Room 13*, Swindells became the only writer besides Dahl to win the Children's Book Award twice. In 1990 his talents for scary fantasy and incisive social comment combined to make the teenage *Daz 4 Zoe* a modern classic.

Young Bob, the lad whose father walloped him for failing his eleven-plus, has become Robert Swindells M.A. (Peace Studies, University of Bradford), respected and popular author of over thirty books. Wouldn't his mum be proud?

SELECTED TITLES

The Thousand Eyes of Night
(Hodder & Stoughton), 1985

The Postbox Mystery
(Hodder & Stoughton), 1988

Dracula's Castle
(Doubleday), 1990

Hydra
(Doubleday), 1991

The Outfit series
(Scholastic), from 1992

Inside the Worm
(Doubleday), 1993

AUTHOR

119

Jean Ure

There was never any doubt that Jean Ure would be a writer, although her first great work, at six, was not much more than a list of her favourite girls' names.

She wrote another at fifteen which was published by a major firm (and reissued twenty-five years later!). Happily convinced that dreams do come true, she scorned university and left school – only to find herself miserable as an office dogsbody. Today that schoolgirl looks over the shoulders of all her characters who are trying to decide whether to tough out their education.

Jean was born in Caterham, Surrey, and went to school in Croydon. Some of her feelings echo in *The You-Two*, about two first-form girls from conflicting backgrounds who are drawn together by loneliness. "I went through something of that. I went to a small private school, and then at eleven went for two terms to a sort of comprehensive, and I remember the terrible turmoil in my mind."

It was partly her childhood uncertainties that drew her to writing. "When I was young, I was isolationist, introverted, worried, and I found solace in books. Now I would like to offer that same solace to others." She used to be shy, and still ducks out of noisy parties, but she enjoys giving "somewhat irreverent" talks in schools and can be a sturdy fighter, firing off robust letters for causes she cares about, like children's literature or animal rights. Her philosophy may shine through her books, but she would never allow politics to intrude.

"All I want to do is write *truthfully* about the way I feel. Marianne [in the *Thursday* trilogy] will, I think, grow up to be a strong political character, whereas

Nicola [*Mimosa* and *Supermouse*] will be far more conventional."

She started to train as a nurse, and wrote a "terribly serious" hospital novel. The book was accepted on condition she added romance, so she left nursing to write romances about it instead. She worked for NATO and UNESCO in Paris, which led to her translating popular French novels. She got a grant to go to the Webber-Douglas drama school; she married actor Leonard Gregory, and they worked together in repertory. And she had fun writing successful historical romances under pseudonyms.

All this seems like thrashing around, but in fact it was a twenty-year apprenticeship in professional writing. It taught her the craft of fiction, to plan methodically, to be confident but aware of her own limits. And, most unusually for writers, it led her *down* the age ladder to children's books.

Why? Because, she says, she grew up. "I couldn't see the world that romantically any more. Writing for children I go back, very largely, to my own experiences, to a time when I was not so cynical." She began with the love story of *See You Thursday* in 1981, and has never faltered.

She is extraordinarily prolific and varied – school series (*Woodside School, Peter High,* and a drama school trilogy), junior comic adventures (*William*) and psychological dramas for young adults (*Play Nimrod For Him*), bouncy frolics (*You Win Some, You Lose Some*) and moving tragedies (*One Green Leaf*), fantasies gentle (*A Bottled Cherry Angel*) and brutal (*Plague*).

Though she had sworn she never would, she returned to Croydon. She and Leonard rented an almost derelict Queen Anne house from the Council, which they lovingly renovated and then bought, and where they now live with innumerable rescued dogs and rather fewer rescued cats. Sometimes things work out, even in real life.

SELECTED TITLES

If It Weren't For Sebastian
(The Bodley Head), 1982

Tea-Leaf on the Roof
(Blackie), 1987

Cool Simon
(Orchard), 1990

Always Sebastian
(The Bodley Head), 1993

The Phantom Knicker Nicker
(Blackie), 1993

The Children Next Door
(André Deutsch Children's Books), 1994

Martin Waddell

Photograph by Terry Bowman

If Martin Waddell were a cat, he'd be ticking off lives at an alarming rate. The very night he was born, in 1941, the Luftwaffe was bombing Belfast – he spent his first hours under a steel-topped table.

His seventeenth-century ancestors, Protestant Scots, settled not far from where he mainly grew up and now lives, in the seaside town of Newcastle, County Down; his wife's family are Irish Catholics. So he is a true product of this divided community, who finds it difficult to identify with any one group. He tries to break down the Them and Us mentality that tears Northern Ireland apart in the more reflective novels he writes under the name of Catherine Sefton. (Now surely that's another life?)

The love of a story came early. His aunt and, briefly, his mother were actresses, his father's family included several international literary figures, and his father, a linen handkerchief manufacturer in Belfast, kept a serial bedtime story going for years.

He impulsively left school at fifteen to join the local paper as a printer's apprentice (he was hopelessly messy) and cub reporter (he was fine at writing). He lasted nine months before announcing he was off to England to a new life as a professional footballer.

And yes, Fulham, at that time in the First Division, did sign him on amateur forms. But it didn't last. (His passion for football did, in sparetime coaching and in the much-loved *Napper* books.) At eighteen he found himself in London with no qualifications – except he knew he could write.

Another new life. The score after six years? Some horror stories published *v.* one good novel unpublished, plus thirty others just-as-well unpublished. Jobs in bookshops, publishing, junk stalls.

Then in 1966 came *Otley*, a slick, quick, funny adult thriller, which became a film with Tom Courtenay and Romy Schneider. *Otley* and its sequels gave Martin enough money to return to Ireland, and buy houses for himself and his mother.

Three years later he married Rosaleen. They lived in another seaside town, Donaghadee, where he discovered that 25,000 words was the perfect challenging length for him, and that children's books would return him to what really mattered – story. Tom was born, and David – and Catherine Sefton. "Sefton" had been Martin's grandmother's name, and he simply likes "Catherine"; she just popped out when his agent suggested distinguishing the author of *In a Blue Velvet Dress* from *Otley*'s. Catherine followed with *Sleepers on the Hill*, and life was good.

Then in 1972 Martin, investigating what looked like young vandals running from a Catholic church, caught the full force of a bomb and the collapsing building. Unbelievably, he lived. But the next six years were desperate: they returned to Newcastle and bought the dilapidated guest house on the seafront which featured in *The Haunting of Ellen*, the one book Martin managed to publish. Rosaleen went back to teaching, Martin tried to write and care for the boys, whose company he enjoyed – Peter's birth was the only good news.

But from 1978 stories tumbled out – "biff-bang-wallop" ones like *Harriet*, perfect picture-book texts like *Can't You Sleep Little Bear?*, probing contemporary novels about the Troubles – selling worldwide and repeatedly winning top awards. In no time, it seemed, the tally was touching 130 titles.

Nothing can dent strength and courage of this kind. Even lying in intensive care, recovering from cancer, he was writing *Little Obie and the Flood* in his mind. If ever he can't sleep, Martin should try counting lives.

SELECTED TITLES

The Mystery Squad series
(Blackie), 1984-5

Little Dracula series
(Walker), 1986-87

Starry Night,
as Catherine Sefton
(Hamish Hamilton), 1986

Frankie's Story,
as Catherine Sefton
(Hamish Hamilton), 1988

Along a Lonely Road,
as Catherine Sefton
(Hamish Hamilton), 1991

The Ghost Family Robinson books
(Viking), 1991

AUTHOR

Robert Westall

In 1993, while this book was being written, Robert Westall – Bob to his friends – died with shocking unexpectedness from what seemed like an ordinary chest infection. So this profile turned into a tribute.

Bob was well into his forties before he published a book. He ended by clocking up three or more in a year. Short stories and fat novels, ghost stories and fantasy epics, whatever he wrote, his style was gutsy and energetic, and his plots gripping. He hit the jackpot first go: *The Machine-Gunners*, published in 1975, immediately won the Carnegie Medal.

It shares its vivid setting with several other Westall stories, the bombing of Tynemouth during the last war. This was where he grew up, a working-class grammar-school lad. In those days it was a cosily safe but claustrophobic and prudish community, which he loved but was desperate to break away from – a dominant force in his life, and a familiar theme in much of his writing, especially in one of his very best books, *The Kingdom by the Sea*.

He went on to take degrees in fine art, at Durham University and then London's Slade School, with, in between, national service with the Royal Signals in Egypt. He became an art teacher – "not only untrained but colour-blind, but there's not a lot to do with a degree in sculpture" – and for the next twenty-eight years was a department head in Birmingham, Yorkshire and Cheshire, finishing at a sixth-form college in Northwich, not too far from his last home.

He was also sharpening his writing skills as a freelance journalist – he was grateful to the *Chester Chronicle* for getting him to explain the sculptor Henry Moore in 500 words – and in 1972 was the northern art critic for the *Guardian*.

He wrote *The Machine-Gunners* to share something of his own childhood with his son Chris, who became his most trusted critic. In 1978, when he was eighteen, Chris died in a high-speed crash on his motorbike, but he remained a lasting presence in his father's life and work. Bob taught for seven more years and every child became Chris, so that he never refused a demand, and there was never again a free period or lunch break. It devoured him, but he never regretted it. A darting spark, naughty, humorous Chris, would say to him, "Well done, Dad."

Bob Westall said he wrote ghost stories because there were not enough good ones around, but also because of his son. Chris, passionate about bikes and filling the house with their jargon, *is* Jack Webster in *The Devil in the Road*, and Kit in *Futuretrack 5*, and Kit the navigator in *Blackham's Wimpey*. And Cam, too, with his fighting jerkin and silver studs, in *The Cats of Seroster*, which, though published in 1988, was written before *The Machine-Gunners*. Chris had begun to write an epic himself. "In a way he was still around, and I owed him one." He stayed around – encouraging, positive, brisk – ever after.

When he left teaching, Westall was briefly an antiques dealer: over thirty clocks tick-tockingly crowded his small study, along with dozens of Buddhas and his beloved cats. Cats are influential characters throughout his stories, but he always said they must still be *cats*, not pretend humans.

He published around forty books and gathered several more major awards – *Gulf* was on the Carnegie Medal shortlist when he died. He did write for adults, but preferred the hungry eagerness of children. "There's a weary sophistication about adult readers that falls like a pall across my spirit. Children read books that tell them what they want to know … about love, sex, death, injustice, freedom, honesty, old age, conflict and how other people tick."

SELECTED TITLES

The Scarecrows
(Chatto & Windus), 1981

The Haunting of Chas McGill and Other Stories
(Macmillan), 1983

Ghost Abbey
(Macmillan), 1988

Blitzcat
(Macmillan), 1989

Stormsearch
(Blackie), 1990

Falling into Glory
(Methuen), 1993

AUTHOR

Kit Wright

"I put on a different pair of shoes when I write for children," says Kit Wright. He writes for and teaches both adults and children, and with the same skill and charm, but sees them as separate audiences. Young readers think of him as a humorous, rhythmic poet who's occasionally sad, whereas, he says, "the adult poems have a darker side that comes with experience."

After a roving life, Kit seems settled now in Balham, south London. No cats. (That won't last.) He enjoys children – he sounds wistful that he has none of his own, but adds cheerfully that he has lots of surrogate children and is an experienced uncle – and he knows the power of poetry. He's been writing it since he was six; by his teens, it was already the most important thing in the world.

He was born in Crockham Hill, Kent, in 1944, but grew up just across the Surrey border amidst a family who revelled in books. His father was a gifted teacher who played with light verse throughout his life, one witty uncle "could make up a rhyme about anything", and his mother read constantly to Kit and his brother (who became a publisher). Even his public school, Berkhamsted, had enthusiastic English teachers.

He soon learnt to be funny. Kit is tall, very tall indeed – not, he says ruefully, tall and broad like a rugby player (he was actually a rather good cricket player), but tall and slender. All his life he has heard the same tedious jokes from people who seem unaware of how rude they are: "Is it cold up there?" "Someone put manure in your shoes?" It's irritating enough when you're older – to this day, he dislikes cartoonists who cruelly home in on someone's physical appearance – but it's hurtful when you're young and self-conscious. Like Dudley Moore or Ronnie Corbett who must have had the same problem in reverse, Kit found a refuge in making people laugh.

When he was seventeen, a poet whom he greatly admired came to live in the next village. Vernon Scannell, a stylistically muscular poet (and ex-boxer), introduced young Kit to his own contemporaries, and was a tremendous force in developing his enthusiasm for poetry.

He won an English scholarship to Oxford, becoming part of a group of young poets like Craig Raine, who were perhaps too clever, intense and self-critical for their own good. At any rate, many became almost too anxious to write, and Kit was thirty before he published his first, adult, collection. But in the next ten years he went on to win many of Britain's major poetry prizes.

Although he has successfully taught creative writing for most of his life, he coped badly with his first job in a south London comprehensive. Three years' teaching at Brock University in Ontario was more fun, and led to five years as Education Secretary to the Poetry Society in London. In 1977 he became an impressive-sounding Fellow Commoner in the Creative Arts, a wonderful position created by Trinity College, Cambridge; it was while there that his first children's collection, *Rabbiting On*, was published in 1978.

He puts painstaking craftsmanship behind even the most casual effect. A young collection – *Hot Dog; Cat Among the Pigeons; Great Snakes* – eases itself out only every few years, and anthologies like *Funnybunch* take years to harvest. He has plans for fiction, but dipped in a toe with *Tigerella* before diving in headlong. Don't wait too long, Christopher, because *you're the greatest* ...

We like the way you operate,
Frankly, we like your style.

SELECTED TITLES

Rabbiting On
(Fontana), 1978

Hot Dog and Other Poems
(Viking), 1981

Cat Among the Pigeons
(Viking), 1987

New Puffin Book of Funny Verse (ed), 1993

Tigerella
(André Deutsch Children's Books), 1993

Funnybunch
(Viking), 1993

AUTHOR

Further Information

Some suggestions on how to find out more about books and reading

Don't be nervous about approaching children's librarians and specialist children's booksellers; they have expert knowledge and are eager to encourage young readers to share it with them. Both school and public libraries are invaluable sources of information and ideas, and, despite cutbacks, most local libraries are open in the evenings and on Saturdays.

Two specialist magazines that review books and interview writers and illustrators are designed for adults but are lively enough for children:

Books for Keeps, published by the School Bookshop Association, 6 Brightfield Road, Lee, London SE12 8QF (tel: 081 852 4953)

Books for Your Children, published by the Federation of Children's Book Groups, 7 Carrs Lane, Birmingham B4 6BR (tel: 021 643 6411) These may be available in your library, or your school may have a subscription.

The *Young Telegraph* and *Early Times* newspapers often recommend books to their young readers. Some branches of Waterstones and a few independent bookshops produce review sheets, often written by children themselves, in conjunction with a local school. It's worth asking about such information in your local bookshop - or think about producing your own.

More specialist resource centres are kept at teacher training colleges around the country, or at

The Poetry Society, 22 Betterton Street, London WC2H 9BU (tel: 071 240 4810)

The National Library for the Handicapped Child, Wellington House, Wellington Road, Wokingham, Berks RG11 2AG (tel: 0734 891101)

The National Council for One Parent Families produces specialist booklists: 255 Kentish Town Road, London NW5 2LX (tel: 071 267 1361)

Above all, Book Trust in London offers free advice and information on all aspects of children's reading, and has an extensive reference centre and collection of current titles: Book House, 45 East Hill, London SW18 2QZ (tel: 081 870 9055). Also in Scotland: Book Trust Scotland, Scottish Book Centre, Fountainbridge Library, 137 Dundee Street, Edinburgh EH11 1BG (tel: 031 229 3663).